HARRY HOLLAND

A man of many parts

HARRY HOLLAND

A man of many parts

BY
HARRY HOLLAND
WITH
MARTIN KING

HEAD-HUNTER BOOKS

www.headhunterbooks.co.uk

First Published in April 2007

By Head-Hunter Books

P.O. Box 26066
London SW10 0XP

www.headhunterbooks.co.uk

ISBN 978-1-906085-01-8

Head-Hunter Books

All the illustrations in this book are by Martin King and Harry Holland.
Photographs are copyright of Harry Holland.

Back cover photograph: Philip Sharkey

CONTENTS

I dedicate this book to my children
MANDY, JOHN AND TRACEY

1

DAD PLEASE COME HOME

I was born in Brentford Cottage Hospital, West London in 1942. My family lived in London Road, Brentford end, which is near the canal bridge. We lived in an old four bedroomed house with me nan, me granddad, and me sister. Even from an early age my dad never seemed to be about. The family rented the house and even as a youngster I seemed to spend a lot of the time upstairs by myself. When I did ask mum where my dad was she'd tell me that he would be coming to see me, soon or the next day. The next day would come, I'd wait and he wouldn't turn up. This happened so many times but mum would always just tell me to be patient and that he would be coming.

A few times I'd be upstairs, there'd be a knock on the front door and mum would answer it and tell who-ever it was standing there to "fuck off." I guessed it was me dad, and a couple of times I'd run down the stairs to try to catch him to speak to him and he'd be gone. "He don't want ya," mum would say. "Just forget him."

In my early years I never knew my dad but in later years I got to know him. I wanted a dad so much it was untrue. I wanted my dad badly and it hurt so much. I can't describe the feeling I had inside me.

The first school I went to was Malborough Infant School, which is near Syon Lane. I didn't really mind that school but things changed when I moved over to Isleworth Town Junior School. That's when the bullying started. My sister, Kay who was two years younger than me, was also at Marlborough. My Nan used to spoil me a bit and at times Kay seemed

7

to be left out but that weren't the case we all loved her dearly, as she was a smashing kid, who I adored. I say my sister but it turns out she was my half sister. When my mum had split up from me dad she took up with this fella, George, who was my sister's dad. As a kid all this palaver blew my mind. I couldn't make head nor tail of it. It was so confusing. When we went out as a family, or a sort of family, with George, my sister was allowed to get away with things and she seemed to get given more than me. She seemed to be treated that bit different. For some reason George never used to come to the house. He'd always meet us somewhere and then we'd go off out. I remember going to see the film 'The Day the Earth Stood Still' at The Gomont at Hammersmith. Another time he took us for a day out down to Southend. We went there a few times and we'd always go into Rose's Café and I was allowed egg and chips, which in them days was a big treat. At the time I didn't mind George but I always felt left out and at times I felt a bit of a loner. My mum was always slagging my dad off and then one day she dropped the bombshell that her and dad were now divorced. In them days divorce was frowned upon but still dad would come to the house to try to see me. She would always tell him to "fuck off" though and shout and scream at him. I don't know if he knew about George. I can't even remember the first time I ever spoke to my dad and spent some time alone with him. It was only in later years that we really got to know one another.

I remember going around to my Nan and granddad's, which was my dad's, mum and dad. I was about 9 or 10 and I'd jump on a trolley bus and go and visit them. They lived near my school in Isleworth. They'd give me a couple of bob and feed me up and then I'd go around the corner to my dad's sister, Aunt Til, and she'd drop me a few coppers. Money in them days was very scarce so it was nice to have a few coins jangling in my pockets. They always made me more than welcome. In later years, a couple of times I'd bumped into my dad at Nan and granddad's. Later on he re-married and had two girls who to this day think the world of me and I do them. Year's later mum also re-married and the bloke she married already had a son, named Jeff and when my step-dad died in later years he cut me out of his will. But Jeff being the perfect gentleman, wasn't happy about that so in the end I was included and the will was split three ways instead of two. So my family seemed to grow and grow.

Mum sometimes took her anger out on me. When I was a kid I remember one time she whacked me over the head with a stiletto shoe and split my head open. There was blood everywhere. Another time she tried to suffocate me with a pillow and my Nan pulled her off and saved me. That wasn't my only brush with death. As a kid I was evacuated during the war, up to Liverpool. Most kids went down to Cornwall or Devon or Wales. Me, I was sent to Liverpool which was bombed nearly as much as London. I tell ya, I'm one unlucky fucker. I was only up there a couple of days and ventured out to play in the street when I was surrounded by the local kids who said they couldn't understand my accent. They tied me to a lamppost and threatened to pour paint over me and throw stones at me. I was frightened out of my life. After the war me and my Auntie Eileen went back to visit the family I'd stayed with in Liverpool but we hit a bit of a snag when we got up there as we couldn't remember their address!

Another dice with death was when I was playing on a bomb site, which were all over London at that time. I was climbing over the roof and slipped and a rusty nail dug right into by body and ripped my shirt and flesh wide open, but the shirt saved the fall and I lived to tell the tale.

Bomb sites were dangerous places and one time I was playing on one near my house and I trod on a lump of wood with a nail sticking out of it and it went right through my shoe and into the sole of my foot. My mum went mad. She was a strict woman but she did manage to put food on the table most days. Times were hard and meals some days were bread and dripping, which was the fat off of cooked meat spread over a piece of bread and butter, and if I was really lucky I'd get bread with jam. Even with no money I must say she always clothed us well and taught us manners. She was a small, tidy woman that looked after herself well and looking back times must have been hard for her.

It was really my Gran; Elizabeth that bought my sister and me up as mum had a job in the local Gillette factory. Gran also bought my mum's sisters' kids up as well. After school the house would be full with children all starving hungry and full of mischief. Nan was the old school. She was tough but fair. As a young woman she'd worked on the barges on the Thames. My granddad had a big leather belt and if you misbehaved he'd take it off, but funnily enough I never remember him hitting any of us kids with it. He loved his bet on the dogs and the horses and if he had a win he'd treat us kids to some Jelly Babies or a lump of toffee. As a small child I can remember sitting on his knee while he listened to the Sugar Ray Robinson, Randolph Turpin fight. That was my very first taste of boxing.

At school things went from bad to worse. I found myself lying to the other kids. They'd say they were off to watch football with their dads and I'd say things like, I was going to watch local side Brentford with my dad. "You aint got a dad," they'd taunt me, and they'd stand around jeering and taking the mick. "Yes I have got a dad," I'd reply. I got untold shit from the other kids about not having a dad. It was soul destroying. I wouldn't wish the way I felt on anyone. The times I came home from school with the shirt ripped off my back where I'd been fighting. In the end I dreaded going to school. I really had no one to turn to.

I didn't have many friends in school but out of school I had a mate called Jeff Johnston. We first met when I was about five and we're still friends to this day. The Kelly family, who lived next door to me, owned the local pub and the café and me and Jeff reckoned in later life that Horace Kelly, the old man, was knocking both our mums off. My mum used to slag off Jeff's mum and Geoff's mum used to bad mouth my mum and both of them would have a twinkle in the eye when they spotted randy old Horace. A couple of times Horace took Jeff and me into the café and gave us a free slap up meal. Was that a bit of guilt on his part? Me and Jeff got up to all sorts together and even though he never really bullied me he always made the decisions on what we did, where we went and what we'd get up to. He was the stronger one out of the two of us and I just followed his orders. It was nice just to have a friend. I didn't want to row or fight with him as I didn't want to upset the apple cart. We used to play in a place called Field Lane and we'd make shelters and camps down there and play Cowboys and Indians. I'd some times take the Cowboy thing a bit too far at times. And I remember my mum giving me a telling off for running along side the tram and trying to hold it up with a plastic gun and a bullwhip and one of mum's friends was on board, and asked mum if the mad kid that chased the tram was anything to do with her? Years later I recounted that story to my son John but slipped in that at the time I was 21. He wasn't impressed. I'd go for walks along the towpaths and find ducks eggs and take them home, cook them and eat them. Life was so different in those days. As a youngster I joined the first aid cadets a sort of St John Ambulance. Me and me mate at the time Alfie Horn even met Walt Disney at Heathrow Airport, and appeared in the local paper. Later on in life Alfie became a top class burglar, one of the best in the business.

A couple of times my Nan came up the school to sort out the bullies. She was only a small woman but was as game as fuck. One bully was the teacher Mr. Osbourne, he had two canes which he used for punishment he named them 'Little Tich and Big Tich and he was brutal with them. He'd pull your trousers and pants down and before he went about canning you he'd caress and play with the cheeks of your bum. Another nonce case the world at that time seemed to be full of them. The thing is I never had anyone show me how to hold my hands up or how to shape up and how to box. There were no men in my life. I didn't know how to fight. I was getting slaughtered. The other kids had their dads or their older brothers showing them how to fight. I just wanted my dad to be my dad and to love me and to teach me things. I just wanted to be like all the other kids.

2

DIRTY DICK

After the war everybody mucked in with everybody. People seemed to pull together and tried to help one another as best they could. There was a feeling of solidarity, a comradeship, a sense of a community spirit. If someone died a relative or a person would come to the door with a cap making a collection for the funeral. We were skint but we'd whip round and put in a few coins. The person that had died might not even live in your street, they might have lived a mile away, but we'd still bung in.

Nowadays you're lucky to know who your next door neighbour is, but back then you really could leave your doors open or unlocked and people did leave their front door keys on a bit of string on the back of the letter box. We really did have fuck all to nick in them days; they'd have been lucky to get a duck egg out of my house.

Even in those days I was good at ducking and diving and earning a few quid. My first venture was swapping kids comics. I'd get two or three old ones, torn and with pages missing, and swap them for a new one and then I'd sell that and make a few bob. I was clever even back then. My mum used to make ends meet by taking in a couple of lodgers. Loads of families done it to make ends meet. There was a shortage of housing, what with half of London being bombed, so loads of young men were looking for lodgings. The big, old, four-storey house we lived in had plenty of room but it was cold and damp. It was like a haunted house and at night you could hear the rats scurrying around. Sometimes the cat would bring them in and play with them before killing them. See, even the cat had more toys than me! We had an outside toilet which I blame on me being constipated even to this day. I hated going out there, especially in the middle of the night. I'd hang on and hang on till the morning, even if I was bursting. You'd sit on the carsey and watch the spiders making their webs and in summer wasps would be buzzing around; it was awful, a right shit hole, and most times the light didn't work or there was no bulb in the socket so you did what you had to do in the pitch black. I always had this fear of a rat popping up out of the toilet and biting my bum.

We never had a bath in the house either so bath time was in a tin bath. We'd fill the bath up with hot water and leave the oven door open to try to warm the room up. The only heating in the house was from the downstairs coal fire. There were no fridges in them days so everything perishable like milk, cheese and butter went in the cellar. There was a little room just off of the cellar and I used to kid my mates on that the Roundheads from Oliver Cromwells days used to hide out there. If for some reason I couldn't get in the house I used to squeeze down the coal chute, come out in the cellar and get into the house that way.

One of the first lodgers we had was a bloke called Charlie who was a real nice fella. He used to have his mate Dick come around to visit him. I liked Dick as he was warm and friendly and made a right fuss of me. Dick was younger than he looked and underneath his cap he had a bald head which put years on him. In them days baldness was frowned upon. Men liked the Brylcream slicked back hair look. It was all Elvis and Cliff Richard. Nowadays it's more Phil and Grant Mitchell and to have a bald head now don't mean a thing. It's almost trendy to have a receding hairline. But in them days you covered up your receding follicles with a cheese-cutter. It was soul destroying to be Yul Brynner when really you wanted to be Elvis

Dick worked at London transport, doing what I don't know, but in his spare time was always tinkering with his motorbike. As a treat he'd take me out on his A.J.S. bike and it looked the bee's knees. I was so excited.

13

No one in my whole short life had given me any attention but Dick did. He was so different, he took me to the pictures and he'd buy me fish and chips. He used to tell me that I was a good looking boy and that it wouldn't be long before all the girls would be after me. He boosted my self esteem no end. He made me feel human, wanted, and important. Before he came along I had no confidence. I had a brace on my teeth and curly hair and was the ugly duckling nobody wanted. Dick had a brother that lived over near Watford and a few times I went with him on the back of his bike, to visit them. To me it was all innocent, and there was nothing untoward. Everybody liked him and he was good company. He was exactly what I needed and wanted in my life and was the dad I never had.

In them days I was a bit of a film buff and I used to love the pictures. I loved the Westerns and loved Gene Autry. Tom Mix was another hero of mine. He'd fight 300 Red Indians and not have a drop of blood on him or lose his ten-gallon at. The pictures, was pure fantasy and I loved going. I walked through them doors and them old cowboy films took me to another world. I couldn't get enough of them. If I had no money I'd find a way to bunk in. I used to go to the 'Queens Hall' in Brentford, which was known as 'The Bug Hutch', for obvious reasons. They used to queue around the block to get in there. In them days nearly everyone used to smoke so it was a job to see the screen, through the haze. People would be in there coughing and spluttering. Most smokers in them days had yellow fingers where the nicotine from the cigarettes had stained them, and Dick was the same; he had these yellowish brown fingers and it wasn't too often you'd see him without a fag either dangling from his lips or being held between his fingers.

He also had this way of making me feel really grown up. A few times he took me into a pub and would buy me a half of bitter or a bottle of light ale. In my room I had a double bed and a few times he'd stayed over the night and slept in my bed. One particular night we'd been out and mum told him to stay, as it was late and there was a bed there for him he could share with me and not to be so silly as he was almost family.

We climbed into my bed and almost immediately he put his arm around me and cuddled me. I wasn't unduly worried as I thought he was just showing me some affection in a fatherly sort of way. The next thing something happened, which at the time, I didn't fully understand. The only way to describe it is that I felt his erect prick pushing into my bum. Here I was, 10 years of age, very naive, never been taught about sex, not even knowing what the word "homosexual" meant. The next thing his hand is on my cock and he's playing with it, and playing with himself at the time it was just a tickly feeling but my subconscious was telling me that it was wrong. I was so confused. The feeling was nice but deep down I knew it was wrong. Then he tried pushing himself inside me, and now he's really hurting me. I scream at him to stop and he leaves off. He rests for a bit and then tries again. I'm so frightened laying there next to him in the dark and my heart is beating nineteen to the dozen and I'm frozen with fear. I burst out crying and he stops trying to penetrate me. He carries on fumbling around inside my pyjamas and I now know that night I had my first climax.

The abuse went on for the next four years and never once did he mention what he was doing to me. Them perverts are so clever at what they do and how they groom their victims. They're horrible cunning bastards. These paedophiles have it all worked out. They pay you lots of attention, make a fuss of ya and give ya money. I remember him once giving me £5, which in them days was near on a week's wages for most men. That was the only time he did say don't tell ya mum. He was never embarrassed at what he'd done to me, not once. I was so scared and then one night he tried to give me oral sex and I refused so he asked me to do it to him and I burst out crying so he backed off. Without me realizing it I was falling into his trap. He had a game plan to groom me and it was going along nicely for him.

He had a couple of accidents on his motorbike so he went out and bought himself a Hillman Imp car. In them days any car was a luxury. The next crafty thing was he taught me how to drive. I was only about

12 at the time and he sat me behind the wheel, stuck his cheese cutter cap on my head and let me drive his motor. We done a few local roads and then after a few weeks he lets me drive up into Central London and all around Piccadilly. I even went to school and told all the other kids what I'd done and where I'd been. I was met with the usual reply, "don't tell lies."

I never once told the kids at school or Kay, what was happening with me at home with Dick or did I ever tell my mum. I was embarrassed. He'd groomed me that well I knew no different. I thought what he was doing to me was normal and that all dads did that to their sons. As the years went on I even blamed myself for what had gone on. My head was so fucked up it was untrue.

The thing that saved me was the P.E. teacher at school. Mr. Farthing started taking boxing lessons after school so I went along. We paired off and everyone wanted to be my partner. I wonder why? We had them big old horsehair boxing gloves and the other kids couldn't wait to get into the ring with me, as they knew I couldn't fight. I must have been mentally tough inside because I'd taken all the bullying and abuse for years. I was everyone's physical and emotional punch bag. In the ring I took a lot of right handers until I said to myself "Harry me old mate, you've got to fight back," and that's what happened. I stuck with it, trained hard, fought back, listened, learnt and became a not bad boxer. Lots of kids fell by the wayside and either dropped out or just left. Within a year I could handle myself and now my confidence had improved 100%. I came out of my shell and the boys in the school respected me and the bullying stopped.

Billy Hunt, who at the time was the school hard man, found it hard to get kids to spar with. I used to get in with him and we'd go toe to toe. He was a much better boxer than me and stronger. He was a year or two older than me but I gave as good as I got, and I earnt his respect. It's so strange how things pan out in life because years later, Billy worked the door for me at some of my boxing shows

Back at home Dick, on hearing I had taken up boxing, was keen to spar with me out in the back garden. The years of abuse from him came into my head as my mum came out into the back garden to watch. I bashed the fuck out of him and I knocked the shit out of him. "Take it easy," said mum, "you're hurting Uncle Dick." I loved it. I caught him up his belly with some hard body shots, which winded him, and then on purpose I hit him straight up the bollocks which had him doubled up in pain. But knowing that sad cunt he probably enjoyed it? From that day on he was very careful on what he said and how he acted towards me. What he done to me was never mentioned. It was as if both of us were in denial. The strange thing was that for years after it I put it in the back of my mind like it never happened. I even invited him to my wedding when I got married. It was just crazy. He had this strong hold over me for all those years. I felt used and dirty and at times I wished I'd have killed him and in my dark moments I wished I'd killed myself.

When I was about 16 I was in the White Horse pub in Brentford with a girl and he came over and made up some old bollocks about me being disrespectful to him and being rude and ignoring him. In fact what it was, pure and simple, was that he was jealous. I hit him on the jaw and put him on his arse. People in the pub were screaming for us to stop. "Let 'em fight," said Joe Barwick who was part of a big family from South Ealing.

I even have a photo of him with my wife-to-be and when I told her what he'd done to me for years and what he'd put me through, she then told me that she wondered if he was bi-sexual as he'd once tried to kiss her and pushed his tongue into her mouth. What a dirty no good bastard? I told my wife Jan everything about what had gone on. There was no secrets. I didn't hold back on anything. What went on has affected me all my life. I now realize what he done was wrong and I shouldn't blame myself. He was a dirty no good fucking dog. He died a few years back but I still feel the guilt and the pain. What happened with him has affected my relationships throughout my whole life.

When I was about 12 a girl called Yvonne Cawley came on to me as we were playing over Syon Park. She grabbed hold of my cock and made it clear that she wanted me. I shit myself as all I could see and feel inside was Dirty Dick touching me. I felt sick and ran away from her.

All through my adult life I've chased the women, not just for the sex but just to prove I'm a real man. I wanted to show the world just how macho I was. I needed to prove to myself I could get the girls. I wanted to show off my sexuality. I wanted people to look at me with the birds and say "he's a right lad that Harry." Inside I was aching, my head was a mess. I was crying out for some real love, some loving attention, and not some filthy fucking pervert pushing himself on me. Here I was, a teenager just about to leave school, wondering what lay ahead for me.

3

IT'S A JANIE JONES
ROCK AND ROLL WORLD

I left school at 15 with no qualifications. My mum wanted me to go into the print as she saw that as a good secure job with prospects. I got myself a job at 'Joshes Print.' at 'The Butts' in Brentford. They mainly printed books about horse racing. It had something to do with betting. All I done was sweep up and make the tea. It drove me mad so after about 8 months, and much to mum's disappointment, I left and went and got myself a job as a van boy with Smiths Crisps. I met a fella there called Dave Wells who ended up being my best man at my wedding. He was from a big and well respected family. Dave and me became great mates and at the time he was only small so I sort of looked out for him.

We had great fun delivering the crisps, which were stored in tins, with 12 packets to each tin. There were only maybe two flavours in them days, which were plain and cheese and onion, and inside each packet was a little blue bag of salt. It weren't like the crisps today with squirrel flavours and baked hedgehog and shark and pickle. Crisps then were bland and almost tasteless. We'd deliver the tins to pub and shops and once they'd sold out we'd pick up the empty tins and replace them with full ones. It was almost an art carrying these empty tins out of the pub cellars and stacking them in the back of the van. It was also an art breaking the seal on the tins, taking out a couple of packets of crisps and re-sealing them without getting caught.

At 17 I went to work for 'Walls' who had just opened up a new depot at Isleworth. Pre-packed bacon had just come out and it was all the rave.

I wasn't very good at reading and writing but I was very good at maths, especially mental arithmetic. I didn't need a pocket calculator and as a van boy I was every driver's dream. I'd do all the books in my head as we drove around doing our drops and by the time we got back into the yard at the end of the day, what we'd delivered and sold was added up and written out in our delivery book. I'd run the book up to the accountant's office and then we'd get to work unloading any returns. I taught myself all the fiddles and how to duck and dive. In those days the average wage was about £8-50p so to earn twenty quid a week was almost unheard of. That was top money. Some weeks I was taking home, with the fiddles and what have ya, £130 odd quid, top top money.

At 18 I had me own van, now the sky was the limit. Getting me driving licence wasn't easy but I passed on my third attempt. I was earning that well I bought a year old Ford Zodiac for six hundred quid. It was a classic grey and yellow beauty. It had all the fancy wheels and I even had a record player fitted in the car that played all the latest sounds as I drove along. It was the dogs' bollocks.

At work the fiddles were getting bigger and better and I was earning a small fortune. I had the main man in the warehouse straightened out. He was a strict, miserable git with everyone else but with me he was as sweet as a nut. I used to bung him well and he'd shout and holler at me and dig me out for the slightest thing but it was all an act. He wanted everyone else to think he was watching me and was on my case. But as soon as it came to me handing over some wedge to him he was all smiles and winks. "Cheers my old son," he'd say as he'd stuff the bundle of notes into his top pocket. I got to know Joan and Roy Row a great couple that worked in the offices and I'd go to some wild parties at their house. We used to 'twist the night away there, Believe me!

Around this time I was knocking around with Victor Terry and we used to do the West End clubs and pubs and coffee bars. One place, which was a real eye opener, was 'The Robin Hood club'. In there was a real mix of people. There were gays and lesbians, which you very rarely saw, in them days. You'd read about them but you didn't come across them in real life. We were known in there as 'The Masculines' which were the straight players. You had to accept things for what they were. There was no micky or piss taking overwise you were out. When the gays knew you weren't interested they'd leave you alone. We had some great nights in there. The funny thing was the real butch lesbian birds would let you dance with their prettier other halfs and a couple of times I'd nick their birds off of them.

Alma Cogan, who was a big star at the time, used to get down there. Danny La Rue used to play the piano before he become famous. He had these lovely pure white teeth and what a nice bloke. Kenny Lynch used to come in. Andrew Ray, Ted Ray's son, used to come in and we had some fantastic nights in there. From there we'd go off to the 'Continental Club' which was full of all the up and coming stars and villains. The Blue Note was another seedy club where all the seats were actual toilet seats. Mandy Rice-Davies and Christine Keeler was a couple of the faces that used to get in there. 'The Latin Quarter' was another venue where you'd find all the wannabees and the villains. This whole New World was a real eye opener for me. I had money in my pocket and I loved it.

Victor always loved a ruck and what we used to do was I'd entice one of the queers from a club to come down a back alley with me and Victor would leap out of the shadows and we'd rob them. I'm ashamed of that now but at the time I was looking for revenge for what happened to me as a kid. It was this macho thing again. I even visited a prostitute and paid her a fiver and went down an alleyway with her. I dropped me strides around my ankles and fumbled around trying to get inside her when she shouted "police, police," and took off. I'm running behind with my trousers dragging along the floor, tripping me up, and she'd had me money and was off. What a con? Who can you trust?

This wasn't my first sexual experience with a female. I'd fiddled about with girls at school and over the park, and I'd got engaged at 16 to June Butcher. We'd met at the 'Rock and Roll' night held at Smiths Crisps every Thursday. She was four years older then me and we went out for about a year before we got engaged. We had a big party, and mum couldn't wait to get rid of me. But it didn't last, she later married Tony O'Brien who was a mate of mine. 'The Brush and Pallet' was a club where at midnight a naked bird would come out and lay on the stage while so called artists would sit at a canvas and paint her. Me and a few mates used to get in there and just sit there and stare at her minge and tits. Up until midnight you'd have a band on and a bit of entertainment but the main attraction was this naked woman. She just used to lay there showing off her bits and not moving a muscle. All us Herberts loved it. We couldn't paint to save our lives but we were world champion wankers when we got home.

Every night of the week I was out on the piss up the West End. I wore good quality suits and was a real Jack the Lad. I'd have my suits made by Toby Norman up at Wood Green. I'd pick the material, get measured up and maybe have two suits at a time made. It was twenty quid a suit but what a great tailor. He always done a first class job. I looked the bollocks. I'd buy a nice shirt and tie to go with it so that everything matched. Many a time I'd have people come up to me and ask where I'd got my suit. I was on nodding terms with a lot of the serious faces around town. I'd often see Freddie Foreman, Joey Plye, Charlie Kray and others, and over the years I got to know them well. Around this time I met a lovely girl by the name of Maria she was a real stunner from Luton. She'd won a beauty contest at Butlins and had been photographed with TV star Hugie Green, who at the time was the host of 'Opportunity Knocks'. She was married to a musician, and we used to meet up in London she was 25 and I was 19 and it felt really good to have such a classy bird on my arm. We used to go to the 'Stork club' a well-known villain's watering hole and afterwards I'd drive her home.

Just after the war thousands of squaddies bought guns home as souvenirs and as the years went by many of these fell into the hands of up and coming villains. Some people even kept live shells next to the fireplace. How the fuck people weren't blown up in their own homes was beyond me.

As kids we were given rubber gas masks to play with and they stunk. They were horrible things. You put them on and they squeezed ya head to the size of a walnut. Somehow I got hold of this imitation gun and I used to carry it with me when I was out in the West End. I also had a starting pistol I used to carry. I had a good group of friends, like Dave Wells, Bobby Hutchins, Tony O'Brien, Eric Christmas, Dave Mudge and Dave Taylor, and some weekends we'd throw all our gear in the back of the van and go off to Margate.

Victor was more of a devil than me and he went from robbing gays with me to robbing shops and off- licenses with a gun. Because I was earning well and already had a good lifestyle where was the sense in me going out robbing? I just didn't want to get into any bother with the law.

One day I stopped off in the café at 'Bush Corner' and sitting in there was Vic and two other fellas. "Are you coming with us to do this bank in Worthing?" asked Vic. "No," I shook me head and told them I weren't interested. In the end the three of them went off and done this bank job down in West Sussex and Victor ended up shooting one of the bank guards. Vic went on the run as it was in all the daily papers. It was big news and eventually he was tracked down and arrested as he lay in bed with a bird called Valerie Salter. At the trial he came up with some old story that spacemen had told him to rob the bank and shoot the guard. He was trying to say he was mental. The trial was at the Old Bailey where he was found guilty and he was sentenced to hang. I remember him sitting in my front room just after he'd come out of borstal as a teenager and my mum asking him if he'd learnt his lesson. He replied "Mrs. Holland, I'm never going back in there again. I've learnt my lesson."

Around the same time as Vic's case a geezer was kicked to death in Hounslow and those found guilty were also sentenced to hang. I think Vic was one of the last people to be hung in this country. I went around to see his mum and dad a few times before the sentence was carried out and they were absolutely devastated. I remember sitting at home on the morning he died and I felt so numb. It felt like a bad dream it didn't feel real. I thought of all the good times we'd had together, was he really such a bad person? Why did it have to come to this? Vic was from a good loving family who cared about him. He had more than I ever had. We went from playing in his back garden with a pellet gun, to shooting his next door neighbours up the arse and basically fooling around with it. But I don't think any of us would have imagined him going that step further and using a real gun to commit a murder. Him and me did pull some strokes, and we used to watch people pull up on their motorbikes outside the local cinema, wait for them to go in and then we'd pinch the bikes and go up the West End on them. How the fuck we never got killed or was pulled over by the police I'll never know.

Another time I was with me mate, Dave Stairs who was driving a car and we picked up this fella hitch hiking up the road. He jumped in and we started chatting. "Had a good night?" I asked him. "Yea yea" he replied. "Got any money?" I asked, casually. "No, no, I'm skint," he said. I pulled out the starting pistol I had on me and pushed it under his nose. "Give me ya fucking money" I shouted. He shit himself. "He's lying, he's got money" said Dave, "let him have it." I've pointed the gun at him and fired. Bang! The shot echoed around the inside of the car and the bloke fell to the floor. I looked down and he was lying tucked up in a ball behind the front seat and I laughed. The poor bloke didn't know if he was alive or dead. "It's all right mate, we're only joking," I said. We slowed down and out he jumped. The car was full of gun smoke and the smell of gun powder. The poor bloke was checking himself for a bullet hole as we pulled away. I did feel sorry for him. Later I felt a bit guilty and knew I shouldn't have been so stupid to pull such a stunt. One time I was in need of a few quid for a little business venture and Dave, kindly lent me £700, no questions asked, a lot of money in 1960. He got every penny back but it was a hell of a gesture. Ginger Carlisle and Johnny Raymond were another couple of the chaps in those days that if we needed them would always help us out. Ginger could have a row; he was from Brentford and a few years older then me. I was at Jeff Johnston's party one night with Dave James and got involved in someone else's fight. I ended up fighting in the doorway of the lift with four fellas with bottles it looked dodgey for a bit and then Ginger appeared and decked two of them I whacked the others and I got out of trouble. He really saved me that night. In the fifties the Jones family from Hayes were feared and done lots of the local door work. Mickey Jones a real stocky fella fought Ginger on the cobbles and there must have been 200 hundred people there watching. Ginger was a local hero who had the respect of everyone. My old mate Johnny Raymond is sadly no longer with us but we had so many scraps and rows with people but one thing for sure John would stand with ya till the end. We got into so many fights, far too many to mention. He'd take his coat off and through it on the floor, Gypsy style with his braces hanging down and then he'd get to it. Dave James, was recently stabbed by his own son and as I write this its 50-50 if he lives.

By this time I was half a Teddy Boy, which was all the fashion. Mum wouldn't allow me to wear all the drape coat and the drainpipe trousers and the brothel creeper shoes. I just had the hair cut. The Teddy Boys were looked upon by a lot of people as trouble but I was probably worse than the lot of them put together.

I once went on a train journey full of Teds dancing to Bill Haley the legendary rock and roll star. It was packed to the rafters. He was playing live on the train and I managed to get into the carriage he was actually performing in. I loved Bill Hayley and had all his records. He just had that something about him. Elvis and Buddy Holly were also big stars of the time but for me Bill Hayley was the main man. Who would have thought that years later I would promote him?

I also once bumped into Janie Jones who found fame by going to a film premier topless with her sister. In them days birds didn't get their tits out in public but then again she did work as a high class hooker. I even had me wicked way with her and it didn't cost me a dollar. Years later she got caught rigging the record charts and if I remember rightly she got bird for it. But fuck me was she a good sort.

One Sunday morning me and a couple of the boys were driving up to the 'Robin Hood club' for a lunch time session when one of the lads spotted a girl he knew waiting at the bus stop. We stopped and picked her up and he talked her into coming to the club with us. We had a few drinks and got chatting and I asked her to dance with me. As we got to the edge of the dance floor she tripped and I grabbed her and saved her from going over. Years later I married her and I always teased her on how she really fell for me. It also turned out that June Butcher who I'd once been engaged to was her cousin, and we even ended up one time living on the same estate. But in some ways, looking back, living there were some of the best days of my life. I had me mates Bub Plummer and Christine, Jeff Johnston and Margret, plus Dave Yeardly and his wife, Jan and sons, all on the estate. We'd be in and out of each others places and have some right wild parties.

4

A BRUSH WITH THE LAW

Every night I was up the West End on the piss and one particular morning, the night before had caught up with me so I let my 15 year old van boy drive on the round. I was fast asleep in the back on the boxes and he was at the wheel and doing all the deliveries. I was absolutely creamed cracked in the back. I was sparko. When we got back to the yard one of the supervisors was waiting for us. This particular geezer's name was Mr. Page and in the yard and in the company offices it was all Mr. this and Mr. that. "Mr. Holland can I have a word please?" he said solemnly. "Yes Mr. Page what can I do for you?" I enquired. "Mr. Holland it's been bought to my attention that you've been allowing your van boy to drive the company vehicle. Seeing as he has no license or insurance and as he has no permission from us to do so, would you like to explain yourself to the head sales manager in his office?"

So off I went to see the sales manager who, in actual fact, was one nice geezer who I got on really well with. In his office he got straight to the point. He told me that this wasn't the first time I'd broken company rules and that he didn't want to sack me but he had no choice. The only alternative was for me to resign; walk away and he would re-instate me in a year's time. I agreed and we shook hands and I walked out of his office and took the van boy over the pub for a drink.

Half an hour later in walks the supervisor, Mr. Page. He looked over at me and sneered and that was it. I saw red. I said to the van boy "I'm going to knock that bastard out." I strode over to him and whack! I hit him straight on the jaw and knocked him spark out. "Why couldn't he have just gone straight home and left it?" I said to the van boy as I downed my pint and headed for the door. I ended up being arrested for that and going to court and getting done for assault. What a mug I was I was earning a small fortune and in one act of pure madness I threw the lot away. I was crazy.

Over the years I've had a couple of convictions for assault and a couple for receiving. I've always been proud that I've never been to prison and done any bird and for years and years I've now been as straight as a dye. Lots of my mates have drifted by the wayside and quite a few of us could have ended up like me old mate Victor Terry. At the time we were all Jack the Lads. I've smashed up dance halls and youth clubs with pool cues. The girls loved us being rogues the more we acted like bad boys the more they loved us. I look back now and I'm so ashamed of how I carried on.

It turns out the girl who fell for me in more ways than one at 'The Robin Hood club' was named Jan and we hit it off almost straight away. She was a good looking girl with a terrific sense of humour. I fancied her straight away. Her mum and dad were really nice people and all the family were very nice to me. Her dad was a scout for Brentford Football Club so we had a lot in common as I hated football. She was an only child of sorts as her mum had had a child before she met Jan's dad. Confused? I certainly was, Jan's Auntie had adopted the child. It must have been something in the air over in West London because every fucker was at it in some way or another. I also found out from my sister that she'd been, molested by George when she was younger. That's why George never used to come to Nan's house. My sister had told my mum what George was doing to her and mum didn't believe her or chose not to believe her so Nan after a blazing row with mum banned him from the house. So much for my mums staunch Victorian values here was both her kids getting sexually abused.

Jan was a hairdresser and she always looked nice. She was a good woman. Anyway, we got engaged and then planned our wedding but we had to bring it forward a bit sharpish when we discovered she was pregnant. We had a big white wedding with all the family attending. In that summer of '64 my daughter, Mandy, was born. We moved in with Jan's parents over in Chiswick and I found myself a job with 'Booths Gin'. I was out of work for a while after the fiasco at Walls where at one time I was earning more in a week than the Prime Minister. I went from earning twenty quid a week wages plus, another £100 a week in fiddles to £14 a week at Booths.

We then moved into a tiny attic flat in East Sheen. It was only one bedroomed and it was that small the cooker was in the hallway. I loved that little place but Jan hated it. We only had my money coming in because Jan was looking after the new baby. Things got worse when I had my car nicked and the insurance company refused to pay out. When I first insured it I stated on the form that it would be garaged. I didn't have a garage so they wouldn't pay out. I was fucked. No more flash car for me.

I then got in trouble at work when I delivered 20 cases of gin to an address and they wasn't there so I left the cases outside the door and they disappeared. I got an almighty bollocking, for that. Who had that? I wonder?

One good stroke I had was when I delivered a lorry load of booze to the docks. The queue to get in and get loaded or unloaded was a mile long and stretched all the way up the road. Then I struck a deal with one of the gate men who, for a fiver, would let me come up on the outside of the waiting traffic and unload my gear straight away, so instead of queuing for five or six hours, I was in and out in, at max, an hour. The rest of the day was then mine so I'd go off shopping or to the pictures or do whatever. I'd then roll back into the yard three or four hours after my estimated times back and cop the overtime. A fiver well spent? I had that scam well wrapped up.

It wasn't long before me, Jan and the baby were on the move. The flat at Sheen Park was a private let and the council had offered us a flat over in Southall. In them days Southall was a mixed area and not so predominately Asian as it is now. We moved into a three bedroomed place in Convent Way where the rooms were massive. It was like a palace compared to where we had been living.

Around this time I also changed my job and left Booths and worked for a large cosmetic company. While I was at Booths somebody had climbed over the fence at the yard and had driven away a lorry load of gin, which was never seen again. Every morning we'd get loaded up and all go and have breakfast in the canteen before we set off. Most of us would leave the keys to the lorries in the ignition. We weren't to know that the security was that lapse that they'd allow someone to sneak in and drive off with a lorry load of booze. Lots of fingers were pointed and lots of tongues wagged as to who had set such a thing up, but to my knowledge no one was ever arrested for the crime.

In my new job I soon got to tumble all the strokes and fiddles. Perfume, make-up, lipstick, you name it and I would sell it. Gift box's was always a good seller, but it was on the overtime that I really made my money. I'd clock in in the morning, do my round, park outside my house, have a kip and something to eat, go off to watch a cowboy at the pictures and then take the lorry back at 8 or 9 at night. I'd do this three or four times a week. I was earning fortunes for doing fuck all. I had one of my Auntie's knocking out the gear at her work to all the girls.

About this time Jan discovered she was pregnant again and my son John was born on the 19th June 1966.

Throughout my teenage years I'd carried on boxing and had about 30 junior fights for the C.A.V. club in Acton. I then moved up to the seniors, but suffered with terrible pre-fight nerves. I had 42 bouts and won half. My mate Colin Cracknall and me then moved to the Chiswick General Boxing Club and Colin soon after turned pro. Colin was a fitness fanatic who could have a fight. I was then maybe thinking about giving it a go as a pro and then I saw an ad in the local paper for a boxing trainer at the Southall British Legion. In the end both of us went down there and to cut a long story short we started a club up.

At first it was a slow trickle of kids coming through the doors. Peter Smith, a good solid kid from Brentford, done well with us and then Roy Hilton boxed for us and then went on to win the A.B.As with Repton, after he left us. Billy Austin, a thin weedy looking kid who had skinny little arms but could really bang, was with us. Paul Keating and George Rabbets boxed for the club in its early days. So did Martin Heardman who was a local boy who came to us when he was 13. Then he for some reason drifted off and went and boxed elsewhere. But he was one of those people that were who could turn their hand to any sport. He Played for England schoolboys at rugby he could play football and cricket he was a real talent. As a pro- heavyweight boxer he beat the then British champion, Hughroy Currie. He used to spar with Gary Hobbs when he was with me. He could have gone along way if he'd only done things properly. In the end his heart wasn't in it and he became a bit of a messer. Not that long ago after he packed up boxing he asked me how he could get into acting. I told him my agency was full up and the next thing I hear that he's not only got into acting as an extra. But he's got real good parts in Coronation Street, EastEnders. He's well respected in the acting game, but that's the stamp of the kid he can turn his hand to anything. So that was the mainstay of the club. Old Billy Stagg used to train the seniors and we'd mainly take care of the juniors. What a scream Old Billy was. He was only the size of a jockey and was one miserable bastard. He only knew one way to fight and that was jab, right hand, left hand. There was no variation in his instructions. He was so serious I don't think I ever once saw him smile. He was the one that first trained Andy Till who later turned pro with me. He was real old school was Bill and he didn't give a fuck. He would stand up to men twice his size and he'd tell blokes to fuck off at shows and wouldn't back down. You had to laugh at him, he was a right old character.

The first champion I had was Grantly Beckles. He was a lovely, lovely kid and to this very day is a great friend of mine. He's 48 now but in his day he won the National Schoolboys which took some doing, and he was a joy to work with. Robin Cox won the Junior A.B.As with us. Paul Keating, one of ours, boxed for England and he had everything. He looked like a young David Essex and was a good-looking boy. The girls loved him. He could hit, he had everything. He was such an intelligent lad. He had the world at his feet but sadly he turned to drugs and that was him finished. Me and Colin as a team had success with that group of boys almost from the off. He was the hard man that cracked the whip and I was the softer of the two. We were the perfect team. The legendary bare-knuckle fighter, Jimmy Stockins first caught my eye when he was about 12 years old. Even at that early age you could tell he was one hard bastard. I saw him box at "The Roehampton Boys Club" he done the kid he was fighting with in no time at all. The kid was petrified of him. Jim' dad, Muggy even asked if I was interested in matching my John with Jimmy if I remember rightly I replied " You must be fucking joking your boy would eat him alive" or words to that effect. Jim had a massive following of Travelers and at times they were very intimidating. I've always had Gypsy friends and find Jim and his brother Wally and Joe Bug and all the rest of his family great company. The Frankhams are another big Gypsy family who I've had a lot of dealings with and they've a great crack. Johnny Frankhams, Uncle Jim was a right character and when my son John won the ' Middlesex Juniors Title' he got the cup that he'd won and filled it up with Champagne and got us all half-pissed. Johnny Frankham could have been a world champion in my opinion. He was a typical Gypsy boy that was full of guts and determination and if he had of trained properly or that bit harder then who knows what he would have achieved? Johnny had it all and is a well-respected man amongst Travelers and boxing people. I also had Tommy 'Creamy' Eastwood who fought Jimmy Stockins in a bare-knuckle fight on a site in Epsom. Creamy told me and Johnny Bloomfield that the fight he had with Jim went on and on and on and that he'd cut Jim above both eyes yet he wouldn't give in, the only way out besides killing him was to give best. He said the man

Harry aged 14 months

My Dad in his army uniform

Me at ten years old, around the time of the abuse

On Dirty Dick's bike

Me getting ready to hold up a passing tram

First girlfriend in Switzerland on a school trip in 1956

(*Left to right*)
Victor Terry,
me, Alan
Griffiths, Tom
Brown and
another pal.
taken in
Southend about
a year before
Vic got hung

Out with the
chaps at
'Dreamland'
Dance Hall,
Margate

The first love of my life, Maria, at my sister's wedding

Me and my sister Kay, 1961

The only photo I have of my wedding day with Jan. Taken at St. Pauls Hall, Brentford

The family

My three children, is
that a smile of sorts on
my John's face?

My Mum at her marriage to Don. My Gran and my kids are there

Zoe Ball's mum with my daughter Mandy, at the Heston Carnival around 1975

Me in 1951

Some of my first fighters: Peter Smith, Paul Hilton, Grantley Beckles and Gary Hobbs

My John at 4 years old

John sparring at the
Hogarth Club

Fred Savoury who
helped out at the gym,
with his boy Dean

The Hogarth boys with the Middlesex Shield which we won a record number of 7 times

On the set of the T.V. programme 'Silent Witness' with Terry Marsh, Charlie Magri, Kevin Tidy, Paul Docherty and Billy Taylor

Me, Peter Snowshell, Trevor Smith, and John Bloomfield

Rocky Kelly, Micky
Harrison and Gary Hobbs

Rocky Kelly training in
Tenerife

Gary Hobbs in 1983 with his 'Southern Area Champions' belt

John Bloomfield, Champ Eastwood, Dean Savoury, Me, Rocky Kelly, Tony Rabbets, Dennis O'Brien and Creamy Eastwood

Creamy with John Bloomfield and me

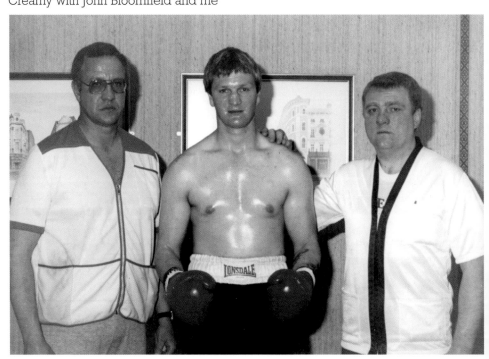

had the heart of a lion. Creamy was a heavyweight who had four fights with me, undefeated. He really could have done something. His brother Champ was a tidy boxer I saw him at 17 and thought he had that something special same with Jimmy's brother Wally to me he was better then Jim in a boxing ring. But lots of these Travelling boys get in other with the Gavvers and Jack it in or end up in prison. Johnny Bloomfield, Creamy and me were on our way to a show in the car when we spotted a horse grazing on a grass roundabout, this poor old horse was falling apart and was a bag of bones. " Here Tom " I said "that ain't the horse, Shergar everyone's looking for is it?" John looked at me and tried not to laugh. We were only mucking about and was having the crack.

" No, no I knows the man that owns Shergar" Declared Creamy straight faced. We fell about laughing John and me and Creamy looked at the pair of us as if to say ' Whats up? With these two crankey Cunts. I had Neville Smith another Gypsy lad at my gym for a while. Neville, Creamy, Joe Bug and Jim and Wally are all related somewhere along the line, but that don't stop them from fighting one another. Gypsy's are born to fight. There was a show on at ' The Café Royal' and the matchmaker; Dean Powell was a bit concerned about hundreds of travelers turning up at the venue. So he asked me to have a word with Neville about maybe only asking his dad and one other to come along, as there was limited space. I agreed and also had a word with Neville and Neville agreed. On the night of the fight Dean powell's all in a flap because Neville's turned up 20 handed " Come on Harry, you've got to sort this out " pleads Dean. So I have a word with Neville' s dad, Wally and give him a bollocking but I get the lot of them to promise to me that if I get them all in then they will behave and keep out of the way at the back of the hall. They all agree so it's all sorted. Then my conscious gets the better of me and I think maybe I'm not being fair to Neville and to his dad and brother, after all they have come to see their boy fight and they are family and they have given me their word to behave. So I arrange for his dad and one other to come closer to the ring but I stressed that they must be on their best behavior. " Cheers Harry my old chavey" says his dad as he gives me a bear hug and a kiss on the cheek.

Everyone's in dinner suits as it's a sit down meal and drink and the Mayor's there and boxing dignitaries and it's all going along smoothly. Neville enters the ring and the bell for the first round goes. Dean Powell comes rushing over, " Harry have a word" as I look over to where Dean's pointing there's all the Smith clan standing around the top table dressed in dealer boots and braces, yelling " Go on my chavey, knock the cunt out my Neville" I just shook my head. I should have known better then to trust a Gypsy. Give them an inch and they will take a mile. But besides all that they've lovely people and you get what you see. I've had some great nights with them and they love a wind up and a piss take. I was at a show with Jimmy Frankham, and my pals John Rowlands, Batman and Ron Ede in the north of England and Jimmy must have changed hotels four times in the matter of days everywhere he went he got slung out every bar we went into he was asked to leave. All I could hear was his young boy saying "dad we've got to go dad we've got to leave" as the kids were getting into mischief and were being asked to leave. Another time we were in this little country pub in the middle of nowhere and we wound these two country bumpkins up to have a wrestle which they did and we made out we were betting on who was going to win. They were knocking over chairs and turning over tables as they moved all around the pub grappling. We were cheering them on and shouting encouragement whilst waving wads of notes in the air. They'd stop for a breather and we'd make out to pay one another on who we'd thought had won. Then off they'd go again. It was a mad house. Johnny Rowlands and Batman traveled to all the shows with me and were great mates, who gave me great support.

Once a year we used to go up to Pontins up at Blackpool. It was a big competition and the boys loved it. It was a big, big show and it was something we all looked forward to. The adults and the kids all mucked in and it was a great atmosphere. I'm a firm believer that boxing instills a bit of discipline in kids. A lot of them suffered with nerves before getting in the ring to box, but I couldn't say anything because when I boxed I must have been the world's worst. I was terrible for it. At one amateur show I witnessed something which stuck in my mind for years. George Dixons, boy Billy got beat by another young kid, and George copped the hump. Me and me mate Peter Dakin had worked our socks off getting all the kids matched for the show. But when George's boy got beat he had words with Peter about the result and the matchmaking. The first I heard about it was when there was a rumpus in the crowd. It turns out George who is not happy as stuck a pint glass in Peter's face. I break it up and pull Peter from the floor and half his face is flapping about and he's covered in blood. It was so stupid we were all mates together. George was a bit of a villain but I was gutted this had happened really over nothing. George ended up getting arrested and went to court and ended up doing a prison sentence. I was down in Bognor at Butlins a few years after that and I bumped in to George and I hadn't seen him since he got put away so I didn't know how he'd be. But we shook hands and had a few beers and he apologized and said it was all water under the bridge. He sadly died not long ago and Peter moved out to Perth in Australia. He did always swear revenge but I explained to him that he couldn't have it both ways as he'd pressed charges against George. Peter was no fool and could have a row and at the time of the fight was getting the better of George.

I think my best fight was when I beat the Army champion, Jeff Yetten. It was in all the local papers and the London Evening Standard ran a story on it and probably my worse defeat was when I took on the local golden boy, Ray Brittle. He was younger and stronger than me and the nerves got the better of me and I got stopped. As I left the ring an old boy in the crowd stopped me and said. "It's a tough game son." Years later I done some debt collecting for the old boy who was too worried to do it himself, so it took a while but I showed him just how tough I could be.

As well as boxing as an amateur I'd go and watch the pros like Henry Cooper and Billy Walker who was the golden boy of British boxing. Henry Cooper fought the great Cassius Clay who later became Mohammed Ali. The first time the two met was at Wembley. The second fight was at Highbury, the home of Arsenal Football Club.

The first fight was the Clay split glove fiasco. When Cooper hit him with a left hook and put him on his arse, just as the bell sounded for the end of the round. Clay's corner bought him valuable recovery time when they claimed a split glove was stopping him from continuing, until a spare glove was found and fitted. Clay's head was given time to clear and he went on to win the fight.

The night of that fight I went greyhound racing with a few pals to a flapping track and they won well and bunged me a nice few quid for taking them there in my motor. Angelo Dundee was in Clay's corner that night as he was for most of Clay's fights. Chris Dundee, Angelo's brother though was the real boxing man out of the two of them. Chris was a good promoter, trainer and manager, and over the years we became good mates every year I'd get a Christmas card off of him. Angelo really got lucky and moved along on his brother's coat tails. Angelo in his appearance and looks always reminded me of an old Jewish doctor. In that first fight the ropes saved Clay because if he had of gone down in the middle of the ring he would have been out cold. The ropes cushioned his fall and prevented him banging his head on the canvas. Cooper could hit. He was a vicious puncher who could take a man out with a single shot. "Our Enery" was loved by everyone, he was a national hero. When he retired I think he got more recognition for his Brute adverts and his charity golf matches than he ever did throughout his boxing career. "Splash it all over" Henry used to urge us in those Brute adverts.

I met Clay when he was over for the first Cooper fight. He was having a training session at Haverstock Hill in London and he was having his photo done with a couple of geezers with a Polaroid instamatic camera, which had just come out. Clay seemed to have a bit of an attitude problem. It could have been all part of his act, I don't know, but as the photo was being taken he exchanged a few words with a black bloke and a white bloke who were obviously, together and good mates. But he seemed to be lecturing the black bloke, "that us brothers don't owe them white folk nothing," The two mates looked a bit confused and embarrassed with his outburst. The British public didn't seem to warm to Clay in those early years. He was seen as a bit of a loud mouth. No wonder his nickname was "The Louisville Lip"

For the second fight with Cooper I went over to The White City Stadium to see him train. When he finished everyone sort of drifted away but I'd noticed he'd disappeared upstairs out of the way. I had no bits of paper on me so I got him to autograph a pound note for me. I wish I had that same pound note now. What would it be worth? He had also seemed to have mellowed a lot and wasn't so loud. Maybe because there wasn't the crowds around for him to play to.

At the fight at Highbury the atmosphere was electric. Before the Cooper/Clay fight had even started the massed crowds were singing Henry's name. "Cooper, Cooper, Cooper" drifted around in the night air. Henry came forward all through the fight and boxed his heart out and caught Clay a couple of times but it wasn't to be. A few years later Henry fought Joe Bugner for the British Heavyweight belt and Joe got, in some people's eyes, a very controversial decision. I've got a picture of Joe holding my son John when he was a little lad.

Years later I promoted Joe Junior's first pro fight. That Cooper-Bugner fight was very close and to be truthful there wasn't a lot in it, but I'd have to be honest and give it to Henry. On the night there was cries of "fix, fix, fix" from the crowd and the next morning the back pages of the papers were full of it. There were nearly questions asked in parliament on the decision. There was never a question in my mind that the fight could have been rigged by the ref or the judges. It just don't happen in boxing. It may well do in wrestling but I'd almost say it would never happen in boxing.

A lot of the Clay fights around this time were beamed back live from the States to certain cinemas in the country. That used to be a good night out for me, Trevor Davies and Johnny Briggs, and Robin Trump, and the lads. We'd go out on the piss and have a meal and then the fight would come on about 2 o'clock in the morning. The atmosphere in the cinema was like you were at ringside. It was incredible. Now and again a fight in the crowd would break out but it was only where some people were pissed and were fed up waiting for the fight to start.

In my private life my business ventures went a new way when I bought my wife a hairdressers to run. She was a great hairdresser but a lousy business woman. J and H Hairdressers we called it. It was right in the middle of the estate we lived on. We also had a little room in there set aside for beauty treatments. At the time there was only sun lamps to give your face a tan, but I got hold of a newly out, all over tanner. These sunbeds were new on the market and people couldn't get enough of it.

It sounds silly but I've always liked gadgets. I was the first person around my way to get a colour telly and people used to knock on my door to come in and have a look. I was the first person to get a video recorder and I was one of the first to get a deep freezer. Sounds silly as I say, nowadays nearly every house has these appliances. Unfortunately my colour telly was knocked off and I got done for receiving stolen goods. Most people at this time didn't have a telephone or washing machine in the house. I always say to people I was one flash fucker, a real Jack the Lad and I reckon that the creator of Del Boy from Fools and Horses must have met me and based Del and his exploits on me. I was the real life Del Boy. Everything you see in that programme I had in my front room. I had the cocktail bar with the pineapple ice bucket on it, the same tasteless wallpaper, the cheap painting of the elephant. I used to have me gold chain hanging out with the gold pair of boxing gloves hanging from it. I even used to get me words muddled up like Del and say things that didn't mean what I was actually trying to say. I could see so much of me in Del Boy, it just wasn't true. It was like watching meself. The only thing I didn't have was a three wheeler yellow van.

In the salon we had a fat reducing suction cap which all the big old birds off the estate used to come in and use. We also had a sauna in there. None of us were qualified to work any of the equipment and one-day a big, fat tart got caught in the fat reducing machinery. She had all red marks and bruises all over her body. The thing is we never knew you had to use water on the rim of it so it slid easily across the body. It's a wonder she never sued us. We gave her a nice strong cup of sweet tea and she was happy. A cup of tea went a long way in those days. A lot of the boxers would come in and use the sauna. You'd often see these great lumps of blokes with broken noses and cauliflower ears walking around with nothing but a little towel wrapped around their waists.

In the flat I did parts of it out with tongue and groove wood but my piece de resistance was a massive big movie screen fitted behind red velvet curtains in the front room and I'd play reel to reel films on my newly acquired sound projector. People used to come around and we'd dim the lights and the only thing missing was the ice-cream lady but Jan used to make tea and sandwiches instead. To earn a few quid I'd charge my mates 15 shilling (75p) to watch a few blue films. They were real hardcore porn. The place would be packed with people some even sitting on the floor looking up at the screen. One night we'd all settled down to watch all the grunting and groaning. When one of the lads full of pre-entertainment beer got up to have a slash, but in the darkness, whilst he's stepping over the sprawled out bodies, he catches his foot in another geezer's blazer pocket and rips it off. This bloke wouldn't stop moaning about his best jacket so in the end to shut him up I had to refund his fifteen bob. It broke my heart I had tears in my eyes. One bit of self inflicted trouble I got myself into was when I clumped, Stomp a local drug user. He was well known in the area as a geezer that didn't work but sat around smoking cannabis all day long. My mate Dave Yeardley came and knocked on my door to tell me that this Stomp had thrown his baby over a fence. I raced out and found him all spaced out, " you bastard I screamed at him" and bang I've hit him straight on the jaw, but he ain't moved, it was probably the best left hook I've ever thrown. He swayed backwards and then looked at me and said, " what did ya do that for?"

"You know why, you threw that poor baby over the fence"

" That weren't no baby, Harry that was my old Hoover, which is broke." After that me and Stomp became good friends and I saw a different side to the man.

Life couldn't be better for me. I'm living like a Lord now. I've money in my pocket with plenty of scams going. Jan and me even have another edition to the family when she gives birth to our third child, Tracey. But an advert in the local paper catches my eye and I just couldn't let a golden opportunity pass me by.

5

YOU AINT NOTHING BUT A HOUND DOG

The money was now rolling in from the hairdressing business. I owned three cars and had loads of time on my hands. Sitting at home one day, glancing through the local paper I noticed an advert for bouncers at 'The Kew Boathouse.' It was a big pub with a dance hall. The Boathouse and The Hammersmith Palais were the two main places in those days for a night out in West London, with both of them renowned places for trouble. I had no experience as a doorman but ended up doing the job with mates, Les Southey, Rufus, Bill Aka and Derek Pearce. But what was good about it was that the five of us almost instantly gelled as a team. In back up we had the likes of Trevor Davies, Ray Hill, Bub Plummer, and Paddy John.

Derek had boxed with me at The Chiswick General and Les had boxed at Southall, so we had a bit in common. There was always plenty of rows to keep us occupied but in the quieter periods me and Les used to chat about our lives and we got on real well and bonded, plus we all had a totally different approach to a lot of other doormen. We didn't cause trouble and all of us always tried to diffuse a situation before it could get out of hand. It was a word of advice here, a quiet chat there, and an arm around someone's shoulders who, was angry or upset. We listened. Right from the off I soon realized that it was only sensible to be polite to everyone that came in. That way if there was trouble the majority of the punters would be on our side. I wanted people to like us. I didn't want a "them and us" situation and I think by being courteous and fair we achieved that.

After a while me and Les between us decided to give this bouncing lark a go on our own. We got four or five venues together and ran the doors and put on bands and a disco but to tell you the truth in those early days it wasn't much of a success and we done our bollocks and lost money. We'd found pubs with halls on the side and agreed with the landlords that we'd run the bands and the discos and whatever we took on the door was ours and they kept the money they took over the bar.

A regular venue of ours was The Northcote Arms in Southall and we had another one over in Claygate which didn't do too bad. One night we put a band on called 'Merlin Q'. They played pop and a bit of rock and roll and they weren't half-bad we paid them for the gig and the lead singer said that if we booked them again they'd get more people down. Apparently they had a big following. We tried it and they were true to their word. Hells Angels and geezers in leather jackets turned up and the place was banged out. For us that was the beginning of great things. The Beatles had basically killed off the old rock and roll bands but we had learnt there was quite a few fanatics out there who still loved it.

We stuck an advert in 'Melody Maker' the weekly music paper for rock and roll bands and through that we booked Gene Vincent, who was a rock and roll legend. He agreed to our surprise to play The Northcote Arms and in no time at all, the place was sold out. Then all of a sudden out of the blue I get a call from Nobby Griffiths, a mate of mine, telling me that Gene wasn't going to appear. Nobby's sister was married at one stage to Vincent so Nobby reckoned he had inside information that Vincent wouldn't show. "You're fucking joking," I ranted, "the place is a sell out." It turns out that the bloke I've got the contract with for the gig was Don Arden who went on to manage Ozzy Osbourne and Black Sabbath. Sharon, Dons daughter is married to Ozzy. It turns out that Gene didn't want to work with Don Arden any more but the problem was we'd already paid Arden 50% of the fee for the gig. Anyway we worked out a way around it and Don copped a few quid for doing fuck all and everyone was happy. Well, in the end the concert went ahead and what a night. It was fantastic. We had a couple of glasses of wine with Vincent before he went on stage. Well, more than a few glasses. He was near on an alcoholic the way he guzzled the stuff. I lead him out onto the stage and it was one of the proudest moments in my life at the time. I'll give the geezer his due he was fantastic. The place was rocking to the rafters and he finished with 'Be Bop a Lou La' and I thought the roof was going to lift off. He put us on the map so we booked him for some of our other venues. We later on had a bit of a row with him over something or other and he never showed at a gig we had booked over in Hendon. One stroke that Vincent did pull on a regular basis was we'd book him to do a 45- minute set and he'd only do a 20- minute gig. He'd finish with "Be Bop a Lula" and then moody that he'd hurt his leg, and come off stage. But I was having none of it so every time he came off I'd push him back on and the crowd would go wild they must have thought it was all part of the act. One night as we struggled with him he ended up singing "Be Bop a Lou La" six times. We also put on Chuck Berry and also the great Bill Haley and had no trouble from those two great pros.

Nobby Griffiths, one day gave me a call and offered us a band he used. "No thanks Nob," I told him, not at all interested. It turns out the band was Roger Daltrey and 'The Who.' I felt just like the man that turned down the 'Beatles.'

With the rock and roll nights going well we booked more and more venues. We had 'The Greenford Hotel' and 'The White Hart' in Greenford. 'The Seagull' in Southall. 'The Fishmonger Arms' in Wood Green, North London. We had 'The Mitre' in Greenwich, where the Dome is now. We also had 'The White Horse' over in Camberley, Surrey. These clubs went by the name of 'The Hound Dog Clubs'. I was earning £200 a week plus. I still had the hairdressers and I used to use mates of mine to help run the doors.

The Mitre in Greenwich was the one place the boys didn't like working. It was a right shit –hole of a carsey and it was guaranteed trouble. When we used to travel down there to work in the car no one spoke a word.

We were so hyped up and nervous about what lay ahead. But on the way home we'd be all happy, chatty and joking and I suppose we were just glad to still be alive. The place was that bad. It was frequented by a gang from Orpington who terrorized everyone, if a fight started and one of their own didn't back them up and join in, then they'd smash them to fuck as well. They were a vicious bunch of bastards. They never had a go at us but we always seemed to be in the middle, breaking up fights that they'd started.

We had a few run-ins with some Hells Angels as well. Their archenemy was 'The Road Rat' motorcycle gang, so we had to be careful both gangs weren't in on the same night. We had a few fist fights with The Angels but we respected them and they respected us. In fact over the years I got to know a few of them really well and speak as I find, they were decent geezers.

To get more acts on board I did a sort of open mike night, a kind of audition for unknown bands. I'd give them a 15-minute slot and give them a fiver to cover their petrol and if they were any good I'd book them for a regular longer slot. One such band was 'The Good Earth Band'. I used them for a while and then I told the lead singer I didn't need them any more. What a daft bastard, and what a mistake? A few weeks later they released a single which was a huge, huge No 1 hit in the charts. Ray Dorsey and his Jug band had changed their name to Mungo Jerry and the rest is history as they say. They were in the charts for 20 weeks in the summer of 1970 and that song is still played on the radio and on adverts on the telly to this day. Another band we used, who done reasonably well, were 'The Hellraisers' who, if I remember rightly, became Matchbox, and had a couple of hit singles. We also had the legendary Bert Weedon who was an inspiration to the likes of Clapton, Richards and Hendrix.

We also booked Wee Willie Harris, who once he put his stage wig on became a totally different geezer! He wouldn't drink before going on stage. Well, he might just have had a little tipple, but once he finished the show he'd really let his real hair down. He was very professional. At one gig the band on stage had gone down a storm and at the end of their set was cheered off. "More, More More" the crowd chanted. But they wouldn't come back out to do a well-deserved encore. Les Southey took the mike and informed the crowd half joking that the band couldn't come back on because the old cow of a miserable landlady wouldn't let 'em. Well, the crowd went mental and all these big, burly Hells Angels smashed the place to pieces. I had to try and smooth it all over and tried to explain to the woman that it was just a joke that had gone wrong and it was just a bit of high jinks by the young crowd. "Come and have a look at the toilets," said the old man. All the pipes and the cisterns were ripped out and there was water pissing everywhere. We never went back there again but Les was right the first time. She was a miserable old cow.

From my advert in the music papers I got a call one day from a Welsh kid who said he'd recently done a gig at some where like, Penarth Pier. I told him to come along for an audition. He turned up and in truth sounded not to bad so we booked him and put him on for a 15- minute slot at 'The Northcote Arms. The governor there, God bless her, painted it up like it was The Hilton Hotel, in Parklane but beneath all the woodchip and magnolia the pub was a right shithole.

One night we had 'Screaming Lord Sutch' on and one of his numbers was 'Great Balls of Fire'. Well, as he's singing it he's somehow set the curtains at the side of the stage on fire. We've jumped in from the wings and patted the flames out. The silly bastard scorched all the wallpaper and the floor and the landlady went ape shit at what had happened to her pride and joy.

On the way to the gig, Les, Rufus and me were in the car and we got into a bit of an argument with a group of Asian geezers. Les has crashed one with a left hook and switched him off. I've sparked my one and Rufus is still rucking. I've stopped him in mid-fight, chinned the geezer and he was out of the game. After it was all over we jeered Rufus up that when he was fighting the bloke Rufus looked like he was ready to take the bloke out. "You only had to hit him another 149 times and he would have been out cold!" joked me and Les. Talking of Les he was a man who showed no fear. It was almost unnatural how he was in a fight. He was always cool, calm and could, most importantly, handle himself. He was never a bully but woe betide anyone that looked for a fight with him. He was a good amateur boxer trained by Jack Hobbs, the old Shepherds Bush heavyweight. Les could throw a left hook like no other man. He showed me the virtue of a good, solid, left hook. He was that good at throwing a punch that he either knocked the person out or he damaged his own hand with the force. He would never bottle it from anyone. He was fearless. He was what legends are made of he was a born leader. You'd trust him with your life and follow him to the ends of the earth.

Another time we was down at 'The Greenford Hotel' and Danny Aylin, a sort of local gangster, who used to hold court in the public bar, was sat drinking with a few of his cronies. There was a sort of mutual agreement that we left him alone and he ignored us. We didn't step on one another's toes. This particular night one of Aylin's clan threw a bottle from the public bar and it hit one of our customers who was in the bar we were bouncing in. I went around there and a big geezer blocked my path. I did no more and chinned him, and it's all off. A geezer then whacks me over the head with a chair and splits my head open. The rest of the boys come around and join in. Les, goes to town on a few of them and they back off. The cunt who hit me gets knocked out as I butt him in the face. It all dies down and there's broken furniture and glass everywhere.

A couple of days later some of us start getting phone calls telling us we were going to be shot. This Aylin character was the type to carry out the threats so we took the bull by the horns. We'd asked around and we found out it could possibly happen. We got a team together and went in a 12-seat mini bus around to where this Danny Aylin lived. Les couldn't make it that day as he was getting married. What a piss poor

YOU AINT NOTHING BUT HOUND DOG

excuse? I knocked on the front door and was let in. Sitting on the settee was a real big geezer who looked like he could handle himself. I said to Aylin "look Danny, I've had me head split open, you got broken ribs and there was injuries on both sides. I've got a wife and kids so let's forget what's happened and call it a draw." The big fella got up from the settee and he towered above me. I looked up at him and for a second I thought, "Harry old son, you've said the wrong thing and it's off now." "That's very sensible," said the Man Mountain and looked straight at Aylin who nodded in agreement. It turns out that the big geezer was a detective who just by sheer coincidence was at Aylin's place investigating this gang warfare. He'd sat there not saying a word and listened to find out who the aggressor was. He told us both to shake hands, which we done, and that was the end of it. Aylin at the time had a few quid and a lot of people feared him. It wasn't all about aggro one day I took this very famous actress out for a drive in my flash car she must have been impressed because we ended up down a quiet country lane with me shagging her in the back of the motor. As I'm banging away a cow in the field we've parked next to as stuck its head in the open car window and let out a rather loud "Mooooooo." I've leapt up and hit my head she's trying to get up but I'm lying on top of her, so she can't move. We've both pissing ourselves laughing. I'm trying to punch the cow on the nose to make it go away and I'm still inside her.

Around this time we had 'The Telegraph' pub over in Brixton Hill. It was a rock and roll venue and none of the locals came in. The local black geezers didn't venture in, maybe it wasn't their scene, I don't know.

One night we had a ruck with some Irish geezers and in the middle of the scrap Les turns to me and tells me he's lost his gold chain. We stopped fighting and us and the Paddies are all looking on the deck for the gold chain. It's gone off again and we do the business and most of them run off with the usual threats of how they'll be back to kill us and shoot us, the usual bollocks. We get one pinned up against the wall and he's threatening to have us all shot. Les looks at him and with a straight face says "Baby, do not mention guns to us because we will have so many guns we will play Ring a Ring a Roses around your house, you cunt, and you will think you are in Vietnam." The mad Paddy must have thought fuck him, he's mental. It all ended happily as Les found his gold chain and was all smiles.

On a Thursday night at 'The Greenford Hotel' we had a disco and on a Saturday it was rock and roll night. One night the Greasers turned up on a Thursday and Les, who loved a pound note more than me, let them in. After a while the boys in the leather jackets said that they didn't like the music that was being played and demanded some rock and roll. The D.J. was threatened and a fight broke out. Me and Les dived in but the new member of our crew, who used to be a pro boxer, just froze. He stood rooted to the spot. He'd been a top class pro and had fought the likes of Joe Bugner. We couldn't believe it. He just couldn't handle the situation. Me and Les had so many bodies on top of us that none of them could get a clean shot on us and that, funnily enough, is what saved us from a serious beating.

The following week we thought that they would come back so we put some pickaxe handles behind the front door and behind the bar. We stood around for ages, chatting and on edge, all hyped up.   But nothing happened. Next thing a mini bus pulls up in the car park, with a few blokes in it, we're straight out surround the motor and drag the driver out, then the contents of the bus spill out. It turns out these blokes are on an outing and have shit themselves. We have to apologise to them and offer to buy them a beer and explain why we'd given them a frosty reception. They could see the funny side of it.

We found out that the bikers that had caused the bother drank in 'The Kings Arms' over in Hayes so we decided to have a trip over there and pay them a visit. Half a dozen of us went in one door and the rest of us burst in another door. We looked around and couldn't see them. It was like a scene from a cowboy film as a couple of old boys sat playing cards, and the barman sat on a stool studying the day's horse racing results. As we were about to leave one of their boys appeared from a little side bar. "Taffey," I shouted, as I flew through the air and dived on him. More of them appeared and the fight moved outside. To cut a long story short, we smashed them. There must have been a good 20 of them sprawled out on the floor. As we were knocking them down Paddy one of our boys was sticking the boot in. He was kicking them that hard he ripped the soles off of his shoes. It was that bad I thought someone was going to die.

Derek Pearce, one of ours, was somehow locked in the pub and the landlord refused to let him out until the police arrived. Derek, who was a polite, well-spoken fella, advised the landlord that if he didn't unlock the door then he would throw him through the fucking window, and get out that way. There was blood everywhere and we didn't drive off until we saw a couple of them get up. The governor shut the pub up after that and he ended up losing his licence. As far as I was concerned that was the end of the matter but in them days I still had to look over my shoulder.

A few months later I was in a pub in Hounslow and across the other side of the pub, in another bar, was Maurice who was one of their boys. I wanted to turn on my heels and walk straight out but I couldn't. I nodded in his direction. "All right Maurice?" I said with a smile. "Yeah," he said and came over. "How did ya get on that day?" I asked, sort of sheepishly. "Yeah, not bad. I had a fractured jaw and a couple of broken ribs and ended up in hospital for a while," he replied. "I'm sorry about that," I said. "No, no, don't worry. We were well out of order," he said, all apologetic.

We did cross swords a few times with the 'Hells Angels' and 'The Road Rats' who were one very dangerous gang. They shot a geezer on Chelsea Bridge and they were not to be messed with, but the trouble they caused was never directed at us personally. Normally we were just caught up in their cross fire.

Besides all that business was booming, helped along by the Welsh kid who I'd given a 15 minute slot to. This skinny kid was Shakin' Stevens and his band The Sunsets. In his dressing room before a gig he would have to have a crate of Newcastle Brown Ale and demanded that a piano be on stage, tuned to a concert pitch. He did get an old piano but he never ever got the fucking beer. Me and Les used to shadow box with him and play fight. We only mucked about with him as he was a lovely fella. I used to say to him in them early days, "if you were born in the fifties, Shakey, you would have been a big star," never for once dreaming what he would go on to achieve. But he had talent, you could see that a mile off. He also always had time for a chat with people. The fans loved him and he loved the fans. I thought he'd missed the boat for stardom but he proved me wrong. He was a real star, twenty-five years after we first met I bumped into 'Shakey,' and I was so pleased to see him. My mate who was there reckons I bruised him black and blue, I cuddled him and ruffled his hair, patted him on the back punched him up the stomach shadow boxed with him. I was so pleased to see him; it just shows ya what real love can do?

The 'Imparlours' were another band who done well for us, plus there was 'Tracey and the Tributes' 'Bill Sheridan', 'The Houseshakers' with Graham Fenton. I asked them to go into the studio and record a version of a song, which was getting a lot of play in our clubs, and was very popular with the punters. It was called 'Jungle Rock' and was discovered by one of our D.J.s on an old rock and roll album. The kids loved it and I offered to pay for Graham to go and record that track and told him I would get him a deal and release it as a single, but we were beaten to it when Hank Mizell, an American artist, re-released it and got to number 3 in the charts with his version.

We had some laughs as well with some of the artists. One night we had Screaming Lord Sutch on at Wood Green. Six of us used to carry him on stage in a coffin to the music of the 'Death March' dressed as undertakers. I'd knock on the lid a couple of times, he'd suddenly burst out and the band would go into 'You keep a knocking, but you can't come in'. He'd then do all his numbers and then after 'Great Balls of Fire' he'd get back into the coffin, close the lid, and we'd come on and carry him off. This time, instead of letting him out on the edge of the stage out of the public eye, we carried him out onto Wood Green High Street and laid him in the road. All these cars were beeping and swerving round him and the next minute the Old Bill have turned up and couldn't see the funny side of it. They threatened to book us for obstruction so we had to let him out and took the coffin back inside.

We had a few scrapes over in Wood Green. One night this black geezer turned up to come in and just by looking at him you could tell he was trouble. When we told him it was a £1 to get in he offered to pay 50p. He was one of them. We made out it was members only and that it took 24 hours to process the membership but he was having none of it. He started raring up so Rufus stepped in and had a bit of a scuffle with him. In the end four of us threw him out but none of us took a liberty with him. All of a sudden we noticed that Les had gone missing, next thing is the door has burst open and Les is standing there with a huge slash across his stomach. We've all belted out and in the darkness we could just see the bloke up ahead having it away. What didn't help was that there was a power cut on one side of the street, so it was near on pitch black. We're chasing him and Les is trying to keep up covered in blood and holding his guts in. We cornered this bloke but he was hiding out in a bush. "Harry," said Derek in his posh, well spoken voice, "flush him out." "Derek," I said, "you fucking flush him out. He's already cut Les up so I aint doing no flushing." In the end he got away that night but the Old Bill knew him as a well-known nasty bastard from around North London.

Les ended up having something like 37 stitches in his stomach and the nutcase ended up getting a four year bit of bird. In court the judge got the hump with posh Derek as he took to the stand and gave evidence against Les's assailant. He waffled on for ages about he knew the bloke who done it, and that the bloke knew him, and that the bloke knew he had done it. We couldn't shut the prat up, it was embarrassing.

All in all though they were a good, tight-knit bunch that I worked with and in times of trouble we could count on one another. The most important thing was that I was earning well and at times struggled to spend the money I had coming in but that soon changed when I took up a new hobby.

6

MAURICE'S HATE CLUB

When I wasn't working I spent my leisure time scuba diving. When I first started I used to dive at 'Littleton Lake' at Chertsey. Les worked with a fella named Maurice McGowlith who I introduced to the sport. Me, Jeff Johnston, Buz Plummer and Brandy and Lime John even went to learn at a proper club but it was so clicky we said "bollocks to this," and went off and played around and taught ourselves. We went out and got all the gear, the fucking lot, the bottles, and the suits. We even bought spear guns. It was outrageous, even in those days you had to have a licence but we all just said, "fuck it."

There was loads of fish in the lake including massive big pike and we were spearing everything. Anything that moved we went for it.

One day a bailiff turned up after complaints from people who were allowed to fish the lake. He told us that the people who had paid for a rod licence to fish there weren't too happy with our antics. "We aint doing no wrong," insisted one of the boys and at that precise moment I popped up from under the water with a fish dangling on the end of my spear gun. "Got him!" I shouted gleefully, as the huge fish wiggled on the end of the point. We got slung off and had to find somewhere else to have our fun. Basically we'd learnt from a book but scuba diving is a very dangerous sport if you don't follow the rules and the guidelines of safety, but we didn't give a fuck. Slowly but surely a few of the boys got fed up and dropped out so Maurice and Pete and me ended up going diving in Dorset. We dived at Portland Bill, on wreck dives. We done all sorts.

One particular dive the captain announced he didn't want any solo dives, we had to dive in pairs. I was used to diving on my own by now which really goes against the rules. The first lot into the water went in two by two and within no time a bloke popped up to the surface on his own. "What are you doing boy?" shouted the captain. It turns out he'd come up because his eardrum had burst and the captain was rucking him for coming up.

Another time, without Maurice knowing, I had tee shirts printed with the slogan on the front "Join Maurice's Hate Club." It was the day Charles married Diana and it was a hot, sunny day and we were miles out at sea diving. As he turned his back to do something I pulled my top up and showed him the tee shirt. "You cunt Harry," Maurice snarled, trying not to laugh as the rest of the boys showed him their tee shirts. Maurice hated everyone or so he made out. He played the part of the miserable, angry git very well. He was the real life Victor Meldrew but with muscles.

Maurice is now a very accomplished diver and is very big in the dive world. He travels the world diving to this day. There's even a plaque with his name on it which is on the anchor from the famous Avalanche wreck. It's in the churchyard on Portland Bill. Maurice was one of the dive team that originally found the wreck.

As the years have gone by Maurice 'as mellowed. He funds all his diving trips by running a reclamation yard over in Hanwell, near Heathrow. He sells bricks and stocks and slates and timber and does well for himself. He also owns a house at Chessel Beach down on Portland Bill and he has met a nice young lady who's now his partner, and perhaps she's helped calm him down. I still speak to him regularly on the phone but don't get down to see him as often as I would like. He goes out on his fishing boat and he supplies half the restaurants in Weymouth with fresh fish. 'Brandy and Lime John' was a character just like Maurice. He got his name from his choice of drink in them days if you were in company and someone bought a round of drinks most people would maybe have just half a lager.

But this John was seen by some as a right liberty taker because having a short off of people you didn't really know, really was a no-no. He as I say was a right character and was always smart, always in dark glasses. But I'm sure if it wasn't for me he would have a got a few digs off of certain people. One summer's day we were with a crowd of people on my speedboat down on the coast. We was all in shorts and having a crack and we came back into dock. He was sitting up the arse-end seeing me back when some how I've hit the throttle and the boats shot forward out of the water and he's gone over the side. We lifted him out and he was like a drowned rat I could hardly keep a straight face. He squelched along the quayside with water pissing out of his nice new suede jacket he'd lost his Foster Grant designer goggles and he was calling me all the bastards under the sun. Me, Jeff and Buzz were in hysterics it was so fucking funny.

Another mate of mine in them days was Trevor Davies who done the doors with me. Trevor and his wife Barbara and two children, Tracey and Lindsay, used to go away with us down to Warner's Holiday Camp. I'd take my kids and we'd stick the kids in the Wagtails Club, which was run by the Bluecoats. My John, being the miserable bastard he was as a kid, hated it. He was one hateful little git. He was never happy in them days. He had no personality. "I don't want to be a Wagtail," he'd moan. Trevor said, "John wants to join the IRA, ha ha".

On the rock and roll side of things I managed to get Shakey a gig at 'The Greyhound', Fulham Palace Road, which was run by Duncan Ferguson who was an old mate of mine. Then one night a bird, who was the producer or the director of 'The Elvis Show', saw him and the rest as they say is history. But rock and roll becoming popular again was really the death of us as a business. We could no longer book the halls for nothing. The acts as they became famous were much sought after. Remember we weren't just the bouncers, we were the promoters. We were making £120 – £130 just on a Saturday night and then almost overnight it stopped.

I was still running an amateur boxing gym and through the boxing, I met some interesting and at times, famous people. I met Adam Faith's brother who used to spar with me. Adam Faith in them days was a busker long before he found fame as a singer and an actor. In his busking days I saw him moved on in Hammersmith and Southend On Sea. He then went on to star with Ian Cuthbertson in the hit T.V. show, Budgie. His brother looked a bit like Adam and wasn't a half bad boxer. The gym, as I said before, was very successful. Grantly Beckles and Jimmy Prendergast was doing well. Gary Hobbs, who later turned pro with me, joined and what a prospect he was. He had everything. I also had the Rabbets Brothers, George, Roy and Tony. Later on Tony turned pro and out of the three he was the least expected to make it in the paid ranks. Tony now runs 'Brunswick Boys Club' and is doing very well for himself.

I used to take them on the pads and I also sparred with them all. I done round after round with Gary Hobbs who was so strong. I drummed the use of the upper cut into him. When he first came to me he was this skinny little kid but technically he was sound and very strong. We had Middlesex Champions, Schoolboy Champions and A.B.A. Champions and then out of the blue we were given notice to quit the premises. Billy went off and found a place but to tell you the truth me and Colin didn't fancy it. Colin then found a place at Chiswick and we parted company with Billy who set up camp in Northott. Funny thing was both clubs kept the blue and gold colours.

The new premises we had at Hogarth was like a palace compared to the other place. We had hot showers and central heating that worked. It was in an old school run by Wally Walsh who ran it as a Sports Centre. Besides the boxing there was a weight lifting gym and a gymnastics hall for the kids. All the kids respected us as we talked to them at their level. We won the Middlesex Shield seven years on the trot, which was a record. An old pro fighter, Lenny Caine from Notting Hill, asked me to take on the Williams Brothers. They were a right pair of scally wags but they listened and turned out to be good boxers. We seemed to attract all the hooligans and troublemakers.

My mate, Fred Savoury, bought his two boys down, Ray and Dean and then along came, Rocky Kelly. At the time he was only about 14 and I told him to come back in a year's time, as I didn't have any spaces. He had a little squeaky voice in them days and a year to the day he came back. "Hello," he said in his high pitched voice. I looked at him blankly. "It's me, Hamilton," he says. "Hamilton who?" I asked, still none the wiser. "You told me to come back in a year's time," he said. I thought, fair dos to the kid he aint gone to another club and he's come back to me, so I said, "right, you're on." Straight away I could see something in him. He had grit and determination and was as brave as a lion. I got him fit and he waited 9 months before we got him a fight. That's how long before any of my new fighters got into the ring for a match, but he was like a little Pitbull. He just wanted to get in the ring and fight. He loved it. I named him Rocky because of his style and to me his name Hamilton didn't go with the way he fought. He was too mean and nasty to be a Hamilton.

At the Hogarth Club there was a great comraderie. It was all for one and one for all. We all looked out for each other. I even had my John boxing with me. He'd been able to hold his hands up properly since the age of about 4. I didn't give him any sweets or crisps until he did the perfect left hook, right hook combination on the palm of my hands. He grew up with boxing. He had 28 fights for Hogarth at junior level and he won 25. Clay O'Shea beat him and Clay at the time was the bollocks. He had won his first 12 fights by knockouts or stoppages and then got beat and turned it in. John jacked it in because he said I was too strict. There was no fucking about with me. I remember I bollocked him when he was about 17 for turning up late and he thought because I was his dad I'd give him a bit of leeway. He got treated the same as all my boxers. Brian Griffths was one of my amateur boxers who has been best friends with my John since they were about 8 years old. He was a lovely boxer with a great left hook who could really punch. But just lately he's been going through a rough time with illness and I wish him well he's a lovely fella. I also had Mark Marriner brother of Jason the infamous Chelsea headhunter football hooligan who's now a very successful writer. Mark was a handy boxer and I was a good friend with their dad who had the 'Chequers' pub opposite West Middlesex Hospital. I was in there one day and there was a bit of a rumpus and I ended up chinning a couple of geezers and sparking them out. In there at the time was aload of OAPs and I did hear I was their hero for a while. I was West London's version of Edward Woodwards TV series 'The Equalizer'

Not long after he packed in he got involved in a fight with some knife carrying Asian fellas. As John was giving one of these blokes a bit of a hiding, the local priest walks by and recognizes John. John was arrested and went to court. It was his first offence but that didn't stop the judge giving him a 6-month prison sentence for affray. His first offence and jail that really broke my heart. In the end looking back it may well have been a blessing in disguise. It straightened him out, and taught him a lesson. He really wasn't a bad kid and just like all of us as teenagers we're all looking for our own identities.

A mate of mine who knew a few of the screws where John was banged up, told me to go and have a word with the screw called 'Fat Eric'. "He'll look after ya boy" said me mate. So one day, off I go to the prison and as the screws are clocking in for the morning shift, I spot a fat bloke in uniform who's a ringer for the bloke my mate described he was just how my mate described him, he really was. He was fat, obnoxious looking and had hate in his eyes. I sidled up to him and in true James Bond style, with the collar turned up on my coat and speaking out of the corner of my mouth, I asked if he was Eric. He asked me who wanted to know and I explained that I was a friend of a friend and that my son John was banged up in the prison and that if he looked after my John I would look after him, no questions asked. His beady eyes looked down at me from under his prison issue cap, which was pulled down to the top of his nose. He jangled his keys on a chain as he stared into my face whilst I was waiting for an answer.
"How do you know, I'm the man you're looking for?"
"Well, if you don't mind me saying sir you have quite a presence about

you." It was all tongue in cheek but inside I'm laughing because I've found Fat Eric and my mate's description was spot on.

Well after that initial chat fair dos to him, he kept his side of the bargain and kept my John out of trouble and looked out for him. I used to bung him a drink in return, give him tickets for fights, and he turned out to be a half-decent geezer.

Long before my John got put away when he was about 12, he came in one night saying to the wife that someone had hit him. I was in the bath and there was such a commotion downstairs I jumped up, got half dried and pulled a pair of trousers on. "Some bloke's hit me dad," he said, standing at the bottom of the stairs, shaking. I storm out of the front door followed by John and half a dozen of his mates. "He's at the tower block," a couple of them point out. "Keep up," says one of the boys to the rest of the gang. "Harry's going to have a row," their little legs struggled to keep pace, as I stormed up the road. Standing outside the block of flats is a bloke. "That's him," shouts John and I march towards him. "You cunt," I growl and held my hands up. "CRASH" I throw a left hook and he moves his head and I miss. "CRASH I throw another big shot and I miss as he side steps it. Now I'm thinking this mug thinks he's Muhammad Ali. I set him up again for a left hook and "BANG" his old woman comes up behind me and smashes me over the head with her high heel shoe. Unbeknown to me, my wife Jan has followed us up the road. "Jan," I shouted, rubbing my head and checking my hands for any sign of blood "get her." Jan stood there wondering what the hell was going on. Now Jan was never a fighter. She was always immaculately dressed and she never had a hair out of place. Her make up and nails were always done and she carried herself like the lady she was. But by all accounts she was a bit of a Tomboy when she was younger. I didn't hang about as I crashed a left hook into the side of this geezer's head. His legs wobbled but he managed to stay on his feet and scramble inside the tower block locking the front door behind him. The police arrived and straight away I owned up to what was going on.

Anyway, they let me off with a caution after I squared it up with the geezer and we both agreed there'd been a misunderstanding. As we walked back home I asked John if he was proud of his old dad. "I've still got it son, aint I?" I said, proudly. "What I would have done," said John "was open him up with the jab and then gone in with a left and a right and then moved in with a couple of body shots." He said this with his usual dead pan expression. He was always very surly looking but what is the world coming to? When the trainer. Is being coached by his boxer?

My two girls have never been like him. My Mandy's as straight as a dye and when she was a bank manager she even told me off for being overdrawn. She was once the local carnival princess and Zoe Balls mum was the carnival Queen the same year. Tracey is just me. She's so like me. She gets on with everyone and loves a chat. She loves her boxing. She's a great girl. John 'as his own gym now and he's a very good coach. He puts in little touches I'd have never thought of. He's making his own mark with his boxers and I'm very proud of him.

Meanwhile at The Hogarth gym Rocky Kelly beat Steve Watt in, if I remember rightly, the London Area A.B.As semi finals. Rocky then went on to lose to Johnny Andrews in a close fight in the final. Billy Austin another of my boys with loads of potential who with his power could near on punch holes in people fought Charlie Magri at 'The Harbour Youth Club' Charlie got the decision on points in a very close fight. I managed to get a return fight after months of badgering and moaning from Billy at 'The Red Lion' Houslow. On the Night I didn't have a clue to how it was going to go, but to every ones surprise Billy sparked him and got his revenge. I still wind Charlie up about that when I see him. When I trained my boys, I trained them like pros so they were fitter than most boys from other clubs were. I'd let my boys spar 3-minute rounds in the gym so when it came to doing 2 minutes at a show by rights they should piss it and not run out of steam.

Two of my fighters, El Edwards and Georgie Walker, had so much potential that they had pro fighter written all over them. Walker turned pro with George Francis. But I wished he had of stayed with me. He didn't do too badly but in the end he fell by the wayside. El Edwards turned pro and went with Ray Brittle and Johnny Bloomfield. I'd first John when he was boxing up at George Daley's gym at Haverstock Hill. Ray I'd boxed myself as an amateur and he went on to turn pro and won the Southern Area title. He was then beaten by Chris Finnegan so that gives you an idea on how good he was.

Me and Johnny after that first meet started getting friendly and we used to bump into one another at shows. John would pop down the gym for a chat and we'd go off after and have a few beers, and if there were no one doing the pads in the gym he'd jump on and take the boys. I had boys then, who looked in my opinion, good enough to turn pro. I had Ralph Young, a great southpaw with plenty of potential and Rocky Kelly who'd just had a close fight with Errol Christie in the A.B.As. Rocky also fought Andy Till 3 times, winning 2 and losing the other, but to be truthful all were very close contests. I had Gary Hobbs who in my view had the potential to go all the way, and I mean all the way. That kid had everything and I seriously saw him turning pro and winning nigh on everything, British Titles, European Titles and even a shot at the World Title. I rated him that highly. When Alan Minter was fighting Marvin Hagler for the World Title. Gary sparred with him and you couldn't honestly tell which one was fighting Hagler. I was also training Billy Hardy for Les Southey who didn't have a manager's licence. With all this happening it was time for me to move on up to the pros.

7

"ROCKY, ROCKY, ROCKY"

Through the boxing I met Danny Mahoney who was the real life Delboy. He was a smashing fella. He used to manage Sammy McSpadden, ex British champion and World Title contender. Danny was always up to something. He was a larger than life character who once had a greengrocer shop off North End Road in Fulham. When I was up to a bit of villianary I'd pop a bit of gear around to Danny and we'd sell bits and pieces from out the back of his shop. One time I had a load of knocked off ladies' dresses so there was a steady stream of girls coming through the spuds and the carrots and out into the back of the shop to try on the latest designer gear.

We always used to sit around talking about boxers and the fight game and he always said to me that if I ever went pro as a trainer or manager then I should talk to him. I mentioned to him about the possibility of Rocky, Gary Hobbs and Micky Harrison turning pro. He explained that I had to get a pro trainer's licence first before I could become a manager. He offered to take out the manager's licence because he had all sorts of contacts in the game, while I trained the lads. Then by sheer coincidence I get a call from Frank Warren. He offered me the chance to go on board with him with my own boys. Warren at the time had just started and he was in competition so to speak with the likes of Micky Duff, Terry Lawless and Mike Barrett. Jarvis Astire was the Mr. Big of boxing. He had all the dough and the main say on a lot of things.

One time Micky Duff wanted me to join him and his stable as his matchmaker but I turned him down. Needless to say Jarvis wasn't too happy and at one time didn't seem to have a lot to say to me even when we mixed in the same circles.

Once a year I had a little minding job looking after the celebrity author Barbara Cartland. I used to go with her to the ballet and there'd be a party afterwards and Jarvis would be there so the few times we did see one another, he had to bring himself to chat to me. I got my trainer's licence in 1982 and went and had a meeting with Frank Warren at his offices at the Barbican. At the time he was in partnership with Frank McClintock, the ex Arsenal player. He had really big plans for himself and his company as he had a lot of self belief. In the end he did crack it and I know for a fact how hard he had it. Everything he got he fought for. He didn't get on with the other promoters or the Boxing Board but he stuck in there and proved a hell of a lot of people wrong.

When he first started he was in partnership with an Irish fella and they called themselves 'Pirate Promotions'. For some reason the Irish fella fell out with Frank so me and him done a joint promotion at Acton Town Hall. At the time he had Terry Marsh, Eugene Maloney, Franks brother, and Gary Knight. We got on really well and Frank and his lovely wife Sue, used to socialize with me and Jan.

We then done a fantastic boxing show at 'Blazers Club' in Windsor. We banged it out and George, the owner, was well pleased. His star attraction at the time was the comedian Freddie Starr. This particular night we had a sit down dinner and dance and the cabaret was 'Chas and Dave'. The atmosphere was electric and there was some terrific bouts. Everyone was having a great time. People were pissed and dancing in the aisles. Birds were dancing on the tables and were hitching their skirts up. It was let ya hair down time. It was a mental night!

I've gone outside to have a chat with the Boxing Board of Control to tell them what a good night it was and on how things had gone without a hitch, when Johnny Bloomfield came looking for me. "Harry, Harry, it's all going off in there. They're bleedin animals the lot of them." And

Johns headed for the exit. I've gone flying back inside and me and Les Southey and big George Cooper, the stuntman, have gone towards the trouble in the far corner. It looked like two tables full of people was fighting with one another. Chairs had gone over, food was splattered everywhere as bodies, both men and women, rolled around the food covered floor, fighting. People were now getting involved who didn't even want to fight. It was like a cowboy film.

Eventually we calmed things down and people were leaving in a hurry. A face, who was a proper face in a top London firm, had been bottled over the head and was none too happy. I won't mention his name but he was fuming and wanted his pound of flesh. He wanted revenge and at one time I swear I saw steam coming out of his ears. In the heat of the battle when he was bottled no one realized who this man was, but believe me he was well known to the criminal fraternity.

I told Frank that I'd go back and see George the governor, as I'd been the one who had had all the dealings with him. I had a meeting with George and to say he was disappointed would be an understatement. He had a list of people who hadn't paid for their drinks and the name of a bloke who'd drove his Rolls Royce around the car park leaving a trail of destruction in his wake. People who were normally civilized had turned into beer monsters. They'd wrecked the fucking place.

A few days later I got a letter from an unhappy George saying that we could no longer put on shows at 'Blazers'. One of the fights that night turned out to be a classic with Rocky Kelly fighting Gary Knight. I felt that Rocky would be too strong for Gary, but what a fight! Rocky had Gary down in the second round and I was that confident that as soon as the ref started the count I started packing away my kit from Rocky's corner, but Gary got up and finished the fight, in my opinion the stronger, and went on to win on points. Gary was from West Ham in East London and wore their claret and blue colours. He was also a big attraction and could sell tickets by the hundreds. Ron Ede who used to own "The Boston Café" at Brentford he supported me right from the

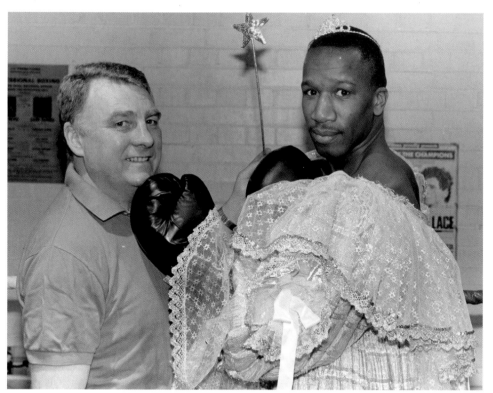

Serge Fame as the 'Cinderella man'

Rocky Kelly 'Who loves ya baby' after the tragic Steve Watt fight

Me and 'Marvellous Marvin Hagler out to dinner

Thomas Hearns, Emanuel Steward and Charlie Magri

Me and 'Ken Norton

Trevor Smith v Micky Hughes

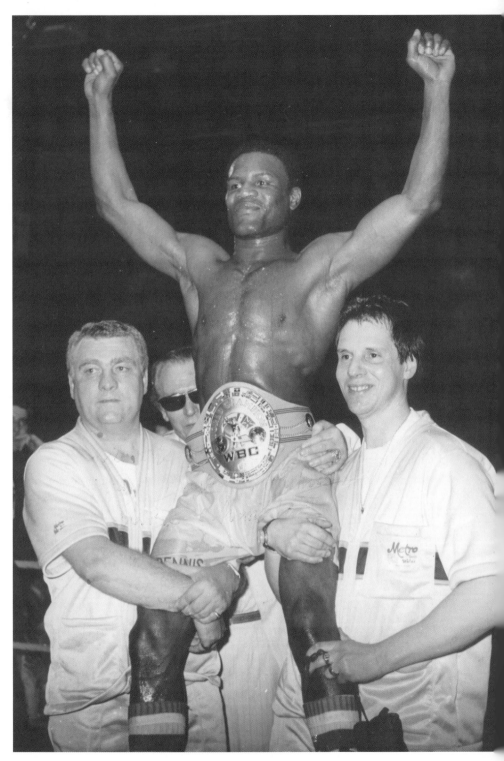

Dennis Andries winning a world title with Alex and Greg Steene

Andy Till winning the British Title with Nipper Reed the man who nicked the Krays in the background

Andy Till with his belts

James Cook and his new bride, Carmel at their wedding

Ladies Night at the Lodge, with Shaun Williamson who sang beautifully that night

This is me with Kara who plays Dawn, with her real sister at the 20th anniversary
bash for Eastenders
A few of the cast from the show at one of my boxing shows

Me and Minty

John (Jim Branning) I showed him how to box

With ex girlfriend, Tracey

With Gaye, a great girl

Madeline and me

Maria Whittaker, page 3
girl and one of my first
board girls. She went to
school with my Tracey

In tenerife with ex girl-friend Tracey. She's now married with a couple of kids

No, it's not Ronnie Barker and Betty from 'Some Mothers Do Have 'Em'' It's me and the wife Jan

Me with the children and their partners

Bill Robinson and his daughter, pictured with my pal Aiden, Dave Evans and Roger Collins. I once boxed Bill and he's since said that he'd never been hit as hard as when I caught him

Me and my John at a party, look at the smile, he's really letting his hair down

My good pal and mucker J. R. Superstar. A friend for over 30 years. I once accused him of trying to chat up Jan my wife when he had an ice-cream van

Maurice, Aka, Me and Trevor, a few of the boys I worked the doors with

Me, Rufus and Aka, 1968 at the Kew Boathouse

Aka, Me and Les Southey, bouncing 1973 at Brixton

Charlie Richardson and Tony Lambrianou. Sadly, Tony is no longer with us

Freddie Foreman and his son Jamie

Roy Shaw, his son, and April, a girlfriend

off. He used to put up the flyers for the shows in his café. He used to come to nearly all of them himself no matter where they was he followed us all over the country. He's now retired and lives down in Middleton, West Sussex with his wife Flo.

Boxing is a funny old game. Rocky went on to fight for the British Title and won the Southern Area Title and Gary also won the Southern Area Title he was also my first pro-champion. But boxing is like that. Great kids can fall by the wayside. They get fed up with the training or they get in with the wrong crowd or get the taste for drink or discover the wonders of birds. It can be a whole host of reasons why good boxers turn it in. If I even have to say it myself I think I done a good job with Rocky and with Gary. No one could ever take Gary Hobbs lightly both in and out of the ring. Only the other day he parked his car only to find on his return the vehicle wheel clamped. He spotted the bloke who'd stuck on the clamp, and to cut along story short roughed the geezer up a bit and then made him take him back to his office where he told the blokes governor, that if they didn't remove the clamp, immediately then he would get the same treatment. The said clamp was quickly removed. Although saying that some boxers can fall by the way side, there are others who go on to better things take Steve Holdsworth the commentator from 'EuroSport' he boxed for me and then went away for a while then he came back and boxed on a show at Watford but it just wasn't there. He probably had a dozen pro-Fights and then I suggested the idea of the videos of the fights and he was the first one to but a commentary with them. A lot of the boxers wanted to kill him for some of the things he said about them on these tapes. He will always help you out and he's got his fingers in a few pies now, so good luck to him. His dad was a good boxer in his time.

It all ended with Frank and me when we had a difference of opinion over something. We were planning a joint promotion. Rocky Kelly was on the bill, and Frank and me fell out and he asked me to return the tickets for the show which me and Rocky had planned to sell, and that was it.

The next time we spoke was when my fighter, Andy Till, was fighting Tony Collins, his fighter, and again we spoke briefly when I was in Audley Harrison's corner for the Danny Williams fight at the Docklands Centre. We might not get on as bosom buddies and I don't like some of his ways and at times his attitude, but I do admire him for what he's achieved. I've worked with most of the promoters, both here and abroad. I go back a long way with Frank Maloney who's another one that's done well for himself. I got on well with Frank.

I've also met Don King a few times and been out to dinner with him and got on well with him. He's a larger than life character. He's a hard bastard and I think his reputation is warranted. Frank Maloney asked me to keep him away from Lennox Lewis at a show because I think Frank was frightened that Don might tap up Lennox to go with him in the future. Every time Don got near Lennox I made up some old bollocks to guide him away from Lewis, but it worked.

At one time there'd been a call to ban boxing as a dangerous sport as there'd been a few deaths and serious injuries in the ring. Me, Frank Warren, Henry Cooper, Don King and a few others had been guests on the Jimmy Young show up in Manchester having a discussion on boxing and was it safe? Don King came across as a nice, easygoing man but I wouldn't like to cross him. You could tell he was a man not to mess about with. If I remember rightly he's been inside for murder twice and apparently he got his trade mark stand up hairstyle by being hung over a high rise car park by his barnet, and he lived to tell the tale.

After splitting with Frank I went it alone and got my manager's licence. The first champion I had was Gary Hobbs who won the Southern Area title. He fought Dave Armstrong on a Frank Warren show. Armstrong was a big puncher and was well fancied. They fancied him 100% but Gary beat him. I'd had Gary from a kid and as I've said before, he had everything. I used to joke with him that I took him from a little skinny school kid to a full blown psychopath! In his early pro days people used to underestimate him. He beat Casey McAllum in his first fight at

Southend and in all he had 10 fights before a freak accident cut short his career. He was working in a packaging firm loading up a remote toy car with another fella. As they were lifting it into a box Gary's end had an aerial sticking up and it caught him on the top of his eye. It didn't actually go in his eye but done a nerve near his eyelid and he was blinded in one eye. I was gutted for him. I really was. He's a smashing bloke who was a credit to the sport. He was like a second son, to me in a way and I sent a letter into support his claim to the 'Boxing Board of Control' when he tried to claim from the injury which finished his boxing career.

Between John Bloomfield, and me, we had a certain way of training our fighters. I worked on the technique and John took the boys on the pads. Me and John had a great relationship. He would never override my advice or opinion and we worked well as a team. I've always had a good team working with me; in the amateurs I had Brian Wells, who help me a lot, along with Fred Savory and Harry Munger, along with Pete Lifscombe and Brian Tough.

Getting back to John we did work well together and we never looked back. A couple of good boxers, Gary Phelps and Micky Harrison unfortunately fell by the wayside. But Rocky went on to fight Kostas Petrou for the vacant British Welterweight Title, vacated by Lloyd Honeyghan. Before the Petrov fight Rocky picked up an ankle injury and somehow I ended up taking him down to Bournemouth Football Club and their physio tried to get it right, but he always seemed to suffer with it no matter what treatment he had. It was never particularly right. The canvas floor in the ring for the Petrou fight was like a sponge, it was so soft. It was more like a trampoline than a boxing ring. I never said anything to Rocky on the night but I knew with his dodgy ankle he was going to have his work cut out on that surface. In the end Petrov stopped him in the 9th round. It was a hell of a fight.

He then had another 3 wins then took on Scottish Welterweight Champion, Steve Watt. Rocky for some reason disliked Steve. It stemmed from their amateur days. Rocky could sometimes be like that. When he fought Frankie Decaestecker at the Wembley Conference Centre which he won in 5 rounds, he then he lent through the ropes and shouted at Steve Watt who was at ringside. "You're next, get yourself ready, I'm coming." You can see me on T.V. pulling him back and giving him a bollocking.

For the Watt fight I took Rocky over to Tenerife to prepare. I think I was one of the first trainers to take a fighter to The Canaries to prepare. I know Nigel Benn has done it since and a few others but I wanted to get Rocky spot on for this one. Tenerife has everything; nigh on all year round sunshine, so the climate is good, and mountains that would get his lungs bursting on them early morning runs. We did our gym work and sparring at Dennis New's 'Spartan' gym. Dennis is a good mate of Joey Pyles and is a well respected man in Tenerife. Dennis is a legend over there and as always treated me with the utmost respect. On the big steak meals and good grub and the early nights I got Rocky super fit. He looked the bollocks with is golden playboy sun tan. 'The Star' newspaper flew over photographer Lawrence Lustig to cover Rocky's training

The weigh-in was back in London at my mate Roy Dennis's pub in Fulham. I got Rocky all suited and booted and he looked the part. I told him beforehand to behave himself and not to let himself down. He shook hands with Steve, looked him straight in the eyes and calmly said "Steve, I hope you're ready for this because I am willing to die for this." A cold shiver went down my back as I thought "fucking hell Rocky, behave." Rocky was cold and calculated, not nasty, but fit and ready.

The show was sold out and you couldn't get a ticket for love nor money and me and Greg Steen, my co-promotor, was over the moon at a sell out. Before this fight Steve had had 12 fights, losing just one, so he had a more then half-decent pedigree. As for the fight it's self, going into the 10th round I would say Rocky had it by one round, maybe two at a push, but it was very, very close. The referee, Sid Nathan was very fair and if one of the boys looked in trouble he'd give them a chance to punch their way out of it and get back into the fight. It was that type of a scrap. Rocky would be on top, and then Steve would come on strong and take over. Rocky would land a good shot and back Steve up. It was a really interesting fight.

In the 10th Rocky caught Steve with half a dozen good, solid shots and backed him onto the ropes. The crowd were shouting the roof down and by now you couldn't hear yourself think. Steve sort of stumbled and looked out of it. Rocky moved in but the ref got there first and stepped in and stopped the fight. I jumped in the ring and cuddled Rocky. I went over to Steve's corner and by sheer coincidence me old mate, Les Southey, was part of his team. I tapped Steve on the head. "Well done son, good fight," I said and went back to celebrating with Rocky. I back looked across to Steve's corner and his head was bowed down as he sat on his stool. The M.C., Dicky Waterhouse came over to me. "Harry, things aint looking too good in Steve's corner. He's collapsed."

In my heart of hearts I just knew before he told me that something wasn't right. I don't know why but I had this gut feeling. I had a terrible feeling right in the pit of my stomach. Our celebrations and joy at winning stopped instantly. In them days there was no paramedics ringside but a stretcher was found and an ambulance was called. We decided to move him outside so that the ambulance crew could get to him quickly and help him as soon as they arrived. As we were waiting by the lift people were stepping over poor old Steve on the stretcher and getting in the lift before us. There was such a commotion but the ringside doctor done his best at Steve's side. Some silly bastards around us were rucking because the next fight hadn't started yet. People were gathering around and asking me as the promoter, as to why the last fight wasn't on.

Steve by now was unconscious and was in a bad way. He was admitted to hospital but died after undergoing surgery to remove a blood clot from his brain. Doctors later discovered he'd been suffering from this for some time and his death was caused by an old injury. I took Rocky with me to Steve's funeral and we went and paid our respects. We had a belt made up for Steve which was the Scottish Championship Belt. I told Rocky to stay by my side throughout the funeral but as expected no-one bothered us. One thing Rocky did do was as the people threw earth down onto the coffin in the open grave he picked up a handful and threw it down so hard a few people glanced at him. He wasn't being disrespectful he was really showing his respect to Steve who he classed as a true warrior. Rocky 'as a heart of gold but he do act a bit divvey at times.

Later on Rocky fought Kirkland Laing at the West London Hotel in Fulham where he'd fought Steve Watt. Laing had Rocky down in the second round for the British Welterweight Title but I fancied Rocky to come on strong in the later rounds and wear Laing down. By round 4 Rocky was coming on like an express train but in round 5 he got a bit careless and got caught again and this time Larry O'Connell the ref jumped in and stopped the fight. I protested to Larry that he was wrong to jump in so quick but his answer was that he could have stopped it when Rocky was down in the second round. I agreed with Larry because as a man and a ref I have the greatest respect for him, but if he had of stopped Rocky in the second I couldn't have complained. He would have been right but in my opinion he stopped it too early in the 5th. Rocky wasn't hurt and he knew where he was and what he was doing. Rocky was getting stronger but I'd give it to Laing. He was a great boxer with a unique style. He once beat the legendary Roberto Duran who a blind man could tell you was no mug.

After that fight Rocky was never the same. Yes, he carried on and had a few more fights, but his heart just wasn't in it. But on saying that he still had plenty of bottle and the heart of a lion. He was fighting Andrew Furlong at Battersea Town Hall and was a clear favourite to win. Furlong had a record of 16 wins, 6 losses and 2 draws. Four rounds went by and Rocky was cut over both eyes and he'd lost every round.

The referee, Mike Jacobs, came over to take a look at the damage and he knows what I can do with cuts and explained that I'd got one more round to sort him out. I sat Rocky down in the corner and got to work with his injuries. "Rocky," I said, "you've got to go out and win this or your careeer's over. I slapped him around the face and sent him out. He got off the stool at the sound of the bell, raced across the ring and tore into Andy Furlong. He had Andy down on the deck a couple of times, and the last time he went down Andy looked across at me and I could read his mind as he said to himself "where the fuck does he get it from?" But that was Rocky. I'd say at the time he was probably the most exciting fighter in Great Britain. If he was around now I'd put him on par with say someone like Ricky Hatton. It was never say die with Rocky.

He had one last fight against Winston Wray at Latchmere Baths Battersea, which ended in a draw. All in all he had 34 pro fights which he won 27 (21 Kos), lost 6 and drew 1. Not a bad record. He was a joy to train and we're still great mates to this day. Everybody he's ever fought has never had a bad word to say about him. The Boxing Board of Control holds him in high esteem and to me he's an ambassador for boxing, a proper gentleman.

So, he finally retired in 1989 at 26 years of age. I wished I'd had a couple more Rocky Kelly's.

8

WINNERS WORLD WIDE

I'd been doing joint promotions on shows with Greg Steen for a while. Greg's dad Alex, was a very good friend of the Kray twins. We'd done well on the shows we'd put on together and worked well as a team but I just felt it was time to go out on my own. I wanted to prove to myself that I could do it all off of my own back.

Eventually I did break away but I had this strange feeling inside that maybe I'd upset Greg and Alex by going it alone. We'd parted on the best of terms but something just didn't feel right. Maybe it was me being nervous about what lay ahead.

Around the time of my first solo promotion Alex introduced me to someone who, the only way I can describe him, as, is fear in itself. This geezer it turns out was a hitman and was being looked after by the firm. I shit myself when I met him and I honestly felt he had my card marked. It sounds silly now but I felt that because of the people I knew and mixed with, and because of the situation. My mind was doing overtime. I must now apologise to Greg for thinking that way. Sadly Alex his lovely dad is no longer with us, but if he were I would apologize whole heartily for harboring such daft thoughts.

Through Alex I met all the firm, Charlie Richardson, Freddie Foreman. Dave Courtney, who's a young version of all the old faces, he's done a couple of good books and is a great crack and is fantastic in his "An Evening With". He's got a great sense of humour but a few people don't understand him but for me he's a sound geezer.

I've known Charlie Kray from my teenage years up the West End and I've had a few good nights with him. Through the boxing I met Paul Crockford who was then the manager of pop group, 'Level 42'. he already had a reputation in the music scene. His partner was Ross Hemsworth who was their PR man and top notch when it came to the promotional side of things. Also on the team was Paul Woolf who was the main man for the legal side of things. Their aim was to promote football, boxing and music worldwide, under the name of 'Winners Worldwide'.

I was signed up as their boxing man and my job or aim was to sign up the best boxers under our banner, be it they be seasoned pros or up and coming youngsters. If I thought they could do well for us I went in for them. I went after Colin Macmillan; young pro with great potential but Colin wanted a £1,000 a fight. I wasn't willing to pay him that sort of money, so we never got him, but it turned out to be a costly mistake for us. As he went on to do well in the ring. James Cook, a seasoned pro, came to me. He'd just been beaten by Herrol Graham and no-one wanted to know him. I told him that I thought he was a bloody good fighter and we put him up to Super Middleweight, but he didn't fancy it. I told him that if it didn't work out I'd drop him back down to Middleweight. He agreed. I had Andy Till, who was a good up and coming prospect with a heart to match the best in the world. He was nearly there. I had W.O. Wilson who Andy had fought and beat. He was in line for a final eliminator. Serge Fame who was ready to fight for the British Title. Carlos Chase, Eammon Mcauley, who were both good prospects, was ready for better things. One time I had 20 pro fighters in my stable. At that time I had the biggest pool of fighters in the country. Vic Wright a light heavyweight from Milton Kyenes asked me to put on a show up there, and true to his word he sold the place out. I've heard it so many times from different fighters who tell me if I put a show on in their hometown, then the place would be banged out. But Vic was true to his word we sold out every seat in the house. We put Joe Bugner, Jnr on and it was a great night. Vic used to travel down every night to train at the gym so there was real dedication for you. I had

Trevor Smith used to come from Harlow, James Cook from Hackney, Steve McGovern used to come over from 'The Isle Of Wight.' He used to do a days work then jump on the ferry to Portsmouth drive up to London, spar, train, and then do the same return journey at least three or four times a week.

I'd have the boys in the gym every night. We had Saturdays off and we'd be back in on the Sunday morning. I classed the Sunday session as a double because me and Johnny Bloomfield would work the bollocks off of them. I used to spar with all my fighters. How many trainers and promoters can say that? and I took a few heavy shots off of a couple of them. I realized after I'd sparred with them that if I'd have knuckled down when I was boxing and I hadn't suffered with such bad nerves in the ring then just how far could I have gone?

Andy Till used to love to crash you up the ribs so that he knocked the wind out of you. Rocky used to love bashing me up full stop but was full of admiration for me for getting in the ring with the boys. I would like to think that all my boys had respect for me. We were one big family and that's how I looked at it. I also liked to look out for my fighters who may have had a bout coming up and that they got all of mine, and Johnny Bloomfield's attention. It didn't matter if it was a normal 6 rounder or a championship bout; the boys with fights coming up got preference over the others. It was as simple as that and that counted for everyone.

One night James Cook came down late and wanted to spar. I told him he wasn't and he done his nut but I told him, "I'm sorry James but next time get here on time and you can spar," which he did. No one got the star treatment, they were all treated the same. I had him sparring one night and he done 4 or 5 rounds and he wanted to get out. I made him stay in there and do more sparring. He got the right hump but over the course of a few weeks he built his stamina up and became a lot better fighter. He went on to do me proud by going out to Belfast and knocking out Magee for the Title. He then beat the Gypsy,

Winnterstein, for the European crown and I then got him a World Title fight, but before he could fight, someone whispered in his ear that the grass was greener So, I sold his contract to Micky Duff for ten thousand quid. I always put my fighters first and at times paid them over the odds.

I flew out to Paris to discuss a fight for Andy Till with the then European champion, Laurent Boudouani. I met with his advisers. In the meeting I gave the impression that I had no T.V. contract to televise the fight and very little in the way of paying out for a big purse. I said I was on my own and had no backing. They looked at me as if I was a nut case. I was completely playing the idiot. I was pleading stupid. I wanted it to go to a purse bid, which in the end it did. I put in a silly bid and you know what? I got the fight. I even managed to get the French champion to fight over here. So, it was all looking good for Andy Till, the challenger. I knew how good this Frenchman was. He'd only lost the once and was, in my view, world class, but Andy was a strong fucker with a great will to win and a never say die attitude. You could never write him off. Me and Frank Maloney done a joint promotion at Picketts Lock Centre and the show was a complete sell out. I really thought Andy could do it.

On the night I think Boudouani had Andy's number and the fight just didn't go to plan. Andy was blatantly butted in the fourth round and it was a deliberate use of the head. A gash opened up above and beneath Andy's eye. He sat on his stool and called it a day. He was fucked. He'd made a brave attempt but he was under a lot of pressure away from the ring. His private life was a mess and his head was just not right for such a big occasion.

I took Andy as far as I possibly could but I will say that if he had of stuck with his day job as a milkman I think he would have been a lot better off. He changed his job and went to work at Heathrow as a baggage handler and the job made him a lazy fucker who sat around supping tea and fizzy drinks and eating cakes, Mars Bars and curries.

Whereas when he was a milkman he was flying around at 100 mph, running in between houses delivering milk. He was the "fastest milkman in the west." He used to finish his job early doors and then be straight out doing his roadwork, and then he'd have a little kip in the afternoon and then be up the gym in the evening. That boy was as fit as a fiddle. I used to weigh him before and after every training session along with all the rest of the lads. They all used to moan and make excuses but Andy's weight was ballooning. He came back after the European challenge and fought the Brummie, Robert McCraken at Watford Town Hall, which I promoted. McCraken's following was made up of mostly football hooligans. When someone spoke about the Zulus I thought about the mob that fought at Rourke's Drift with Michael Caine and Stanley Baker, not some two bob mob from Birmingham. I didn't have a clue about football hooliganism. At the venue there was punch ups everywhere you looked and there was people getting slung from the upstairs balcony. There was more action outside the ring than inside. I'd say it was worse than the trouble at the Hagler – Minter fight years earlier. The fight was shown on telly so the trouble was broadcast nationwide.

Andy was beaten on points and I thought personally he should now retire. It was a close fight but I thought that Andy would now call it a day. The old snap and self belief had gone. He was going through the motions and the way he fought he was as brave as a lion and I didn't want him to get some serious head injury or brain damage. He was too brave for his own good.

He went away for a while and had a rest from the game. After about a year he turned up at the gym one night and said he wanted to get back into shape. He'd told me he'd been out doing some roadwork and said that to be honest he was skint and needed the money and could I fix him up a fight. To cut a long story short I got him a fight with Darren Griffiths at Super Middleweight in a fight the old Andy Till should have won comfortably, but he never. His taste for the booze, the curries and the cream cakes proved to be his downfall.

Looking back at it I should never have allowed him to fight after the McCraken fight. It was a big mistake. Andy was a true champion and had won a Lonsdale Belt outright, but age had caught up with him, plus all the battles in and out of the ring finally caught up with him and took their toll. As the curtain came down on Andy's career so did my association with Winners Worldwide.

After Nigel Benn got beat by Chris Ewbanks we bought him back for his next fight against Robbie Simms who was Marvellous Marvin Hagler's half brother. We put the show on with Ambrose Mendy at York Hall, Bethnal Green. I ended up in hospital with kidney stones after that with all the stress and worry from Ambrose. He drove us fucking mad with his demands. The bits and pieces he wanted tagged onto the contract were unbelievable. How the fight ever got on I'll never know. It was originally scheduled for the N.E.C. Arena in Birmingham but the ticket sales weren't going too good. The poster campaign advertising the fight was of Nigel in army uniform, saluting, with a Union Jack flag in the background. Someone in their wisdom, to save the show from financial ruin, told the police that there'd been threats to blow the venue up, from the I.R.A. That released us from our contract with the N.E.C. so we moved the show to East London.

The thing was the York Hall held two thousand people and the N.E.C. held ten thousand and scatty Ambrose wanted the same money but it was never going to work and no matter how much we explained it to him he just couldn't see the wood for the trees. He was so frustrating. He would argue about anything, phone calls and faxes would be flying backwards and forwards between one another. He even tried to claim 400 quid for the board girl for in between rounds. Normally, off the top of me head, you'd pay a girl say £100 for walking around in the ring showing the crowd the round number and a bit of tit and arse. He tried to say his was dearer because she was a Vogue model. Absolute bollocks.

In the end we got the show on and it was a great show. Nigel won in 7 rounds. We even got Marvin Hagler together, before the fight, with

Alan Minter in the centre of the ring. They cuddled one another and got a standing ovation from the crowd. The past was buried after the crowd trouble at Wembley. That was the first time the pair had met since their Wembley showdown. Not, as the press made out, two weeks later at a charity do which they both attended. That's a fact. They met on my show and had the greatest respect for each other. For some reason or other there was a bit of a discrepancy over the finances from that show. No one was fiddling but some things didn't seem to add up, so we had a meeting with Benn and Paul Crockford from Winners Worldwide. Nigel was very forceful in making a few points and seemed to be winding himself up. I butted in a couple of times and calmed the situation down. Nigel had come with a mate of his so me and his pal left them to it while we went across the road to the pub. In the end they sorted it out and shook hands but for me, that was it. Even Paul became disillusioned with boxing and he said he'd fallen out of love with the sport. I was gutted he felt that way as we'd worked well together.

I'd had some good times with Winners Worldwide. I'd been to Miami with Ross Emsworth, who was a big noise in the company. We had a meeting with Donald Trump to try to get the Chavez, Meldrick Taylor fight. Don King and Bob Arun were in the frame to nick it but we were confident that we could swing it. Donald Trump even commented after the meeting that he admired our balls for trying to get the fight on. In other words, we had no fucking chance.

After the meeting, Tess, Trump's number one advisor, died in a helicopter crash flying back to New York.

We also met up with Dan Duva, Lou Duva's brother, about some of his boxers. We met the Jamaican Heavyweight, Trevor Burbeck, who then fought out of Canada. We hoped to put a show on in Jamaica with Trevor headlining. But we were told, by a government big wig that it would be nigh on impossible to get our money out of the country, after the show. So we scrapped that idea. Technically there was so much corruption it wouldn't be worth it. There were too many palms to grease.

On my travels around the States I met some of the all time greats. I met Ali three times and met Joe Frazier. I've met Sugar Ray Lennard. I've had dinner with Roberto Duran who hardly spoke any English but a lovely, lovely man. His fights with Lennard were classics. Thomas Hearns was another one. I remember he beat Britain's Dennis Andres out in Detroit. A funny story with Dennis was I was in his corner as part of his team when he won the World Title and as we celebrated his win at the end of the fight me and Greg and Alex Steene went to lift him up onto our shoulders and carry him triumphantly around the ring. I'd just come out of hospital with my kidney stones again. As I lifted him up I felt my legs go from under me. Alex saved the day by holding up Dennis by the back of his shorts so if Dennis looks a bit cross eyed in the photos it's because of me and his pants being pulled too far up his arse! It was a great win for Dennis and I'd put that victory on a par with John H Stacey who in the 70s went out to South America and beat the legend Jose Naples for the World Title.

I remember John coming home after that victory and going down for his old amateur club, Repton, when they had a show on at the York Hall. The kids loved him and they stood and cheered him and waved little Union Jack flags. Lloyd Honeyghan was another one who pulled off one of the truly most amazing shocks in boxing when he beat Don Curry. I even let Micky Duff his manager use Andy Till as a sparring partner. No one had heard of Andy at the time because he was just starting out. At the first session Andy was asked to leave the ring so that Lloyd could warm up. That's how arrogant he could be at times. Michael Watson was down the gym at the same time and him and Lloyd had a few run ins. Lloyd could be so awkward at times. Andy didn't do too bad and to tell you the truth looked to have Lloyd in his pocket. He crashed a few right hands into Honeyghan's head and threw a few elbows in just for good measure. Andy began to grow in confidence and looked comfortable and not out of his depth. Lloyd then got beat by American Gold medalist, Mark Breland, if I remember rightly, and was never the same after that. But I just like to think that maybe Andy helped him along that road to retirement.

Since then I've become great friends with Lloyd and he's a different fella altogether. He's a nice man and the arrogance 'as disappeared. As a boxer he had a lot of self belief and he knew what he was doing against Don Curry. No-one gave him a chance but he came flying out of his corner and won the fight. There again Micky Duff's a shrewd man and he must have fancied Lloyd in that fight. He's a shrewd man when it comes to fighters. Years ago he had the monopoly on British boxing and I've heard him speak to some people like shit, but he was always all right to me so I'll speak as I find. He was a gentleman. In the James Cook deal there were no contracts, he just gave me his word, he paid me the money, shook hands and that was that.

I've worked with Micky on a few promotions and he's no different to Greg and Alex Steene, Frank Maloney or Frank Warren, but one person I've never joint promoted with is Barry Hearn. Now he made 'is name with the snooker before coming into boxing and he sees me as a bit of a cockney barrow boy. He's a nice fella and I know he likes me and the feelings are mutual. I watch his face when he's on telly and he's always happy. He's a genuine geezer with a real charm about him, who cares, passionately about his boxers. I've also worked with Jess Harding and Chris Sanigar, Chris, is someone that I go along way back with. My Rocky Kelly had fought Chris at the Albert Hall when they were both young pros. It was a tough fight, which Rocky won on points over 10 rounds. Harry Carpenter the BBC commentator even remarked that a medal should be struck for these two brave warriors.

Me and Frank Maloney go a long way back and in the very early days we were on our coaching course together as amateurs. To past my test on one of the courses I had to write on the side of my trainers the order of the exercises I had to remember. I like Frank but he's fallen out with quite a few people along the way, but he's done well with Lennox Lewis so you can't take that away from him. My Heavyweight, Barry Ellis, used to spar with Lennox and when he was out in Australia doing a book signing and Pam, a lady friend of mine went up and introduced herself to him and told Lennox she knew me, she said he was very chatty and one nice fella.

Recently I was in Audley Harrison's dressing room before the first Danny Williams fight and we linked hands in a circle and said a prayer before we went into the ring, and Lennox came in and joined the circle, which I thought was a nice gesture. As for Audley he's one nice guy and I really hope he gets to the top. He may appear arrogant to some people but believe me, he's a smashing bloke. He's got the lot and I can see no reason why he doesn't become World Champion one day. I'm the cut man in Audley's corner so I see him at first hand and I think he will make it to the top, God willing, with a bit of luck and a lot of skill, which he has.

Another man who I think will get to the top is David Hay. I've promoted a couple of his fights and he's one talented fella and I wish him all the best. He's got the lot too. He reminds me of Trevor Smith, a Welterweight I had who could bang. He went 15 fights undefeated and then got a bit of a drink problem but he was a hell of a fighter who had a terrific left hook. He even made history when he took on Kirkland Laing at the Grosvenor House Hotel in Mayfair and it was the first live fight ever shown by B.SkyB television, and it was for the British Welterweight Title. Like David Hay, he was an exciting fighter.

9

TREADING THE BOARDS

Danny Mahoney had nigh on done everything so one day he says to me out of the blue "Harry, we've got to get into acting." I looked at him blankly. "How do we do that?" So he phoned up the Equity office and told them a load of rubbish on how he had these clubs and that he had a song and dance act that wanted to perform live but he'd been told they couldn't because they didn't have Equity cards. He was told over the phone to send the act to their offices and the Actors' Union would have a chat with them.

So me and him go off to their offices in Harley Street posing as this double act. We go in and talk to this bird who sits filling out a form as we speak. "What do you do?" she asks looking at us. "A song and dance act," replies Danny. "I can't really sing for you today love, I've got laryngitis," I croaked, kidding her. With that Danny jumped up, stuck a red fez on his head like Tommy Cooper used to wear and ran around the room singing 'When Irish Eyes are smiling.' It was so fucking ridiculous. He must have been 60 at the time and I didn't know he had so much energy, and where he'd got the hat from I'll never know. He never mentioned it to me on the way in. We hadn't rehearsed or, come to that, even spoke about what we were going to do.

It must have worked because she gave us a provisional licence. As she spoke Danny detected that she had an accent. "Where are you from dear?" he asked. "Aberdeen," she replied in her soft, Scottish brogue. "Aberdeen? Harry, remember when we performed at The Empire in Aberdeen?" I nodded in agreement. "Don't push ya luck Dan," I'm thinking. "I know it well," she said. I was sat there trying to work out who was the biggest liar out of the two!

We were now the proud owners of Equity cards and were members of the Actors' Union. I did little bits and pieces with it, just walk on and a bit of background extra work, but nothing to write home about. I then got talking to Ron Fairbrother who'd written a book called 'The Enforcer'. I've always got on well with Ron who used to run a cab hire business in Elstree Studios. It's funny how life goes. An older women originally owned the company with her partner who done her for the money and fucked off to Spain. Ron, being a right ladies' man at the time, comes along and helps her out of trouble. Someone from the firm goes out to Spain where a gun is held under the runaway's chin and surprise, surprise, the money is returned to its rightful owner, safely. So, Ron being the perfect gentleman wines and dines and courts the bird and becomes half owner of the cab company.

As I say, one day we're chatting and I mention to him that I have an Equity card.
    "They're like gold dust," he says.
    "But," I added, "it might have run out."
    "Well phone up and find out,"
    "No, it aint worth it,"
    "You ain't got nothing to lose,"
    "You phone them then,"
So he did and made out he was me.
    "Where have you been for the last 10 years?" said the voice at the other end of the phone.
    Ron gave them this cock and bull story about being in prison for manslaughter and that he wanted to rehabilitate himself.
    "What about all the unpaid dues you owe?" he was asked.
    "I told ya, I've been in nick so how could I have paid the money?"
    "O.K., pay us 60 quid and we will settle for that and we'll issue you with a new Equity card"
    So, I paid the 60 quid, which was a bargain. I also had to use my own

name on the card, or a stage name. I used Chuck Connors's character's name Jason McCord from 'The Rifleman' cowboy show on T.V. I used that for a while and then went back to being Harry Holland.

My mate, Bruce Wells, who was a well known ducker and diver and had even done time for fraud, had been selling ringside seats at Micky Duff's shows for near on peanuts but the punters never ever got their cheap tickets. The oldest trick in the book. Anyway, he put me on to an actors' agency just off of Leicester Square. I put my name down on their books and the first job I got through them was a part in the vets series 'All Creatures Great and Small' and to be truthful, I aint an animal lover. Although I have had my share of old dogs. Bruce was also one of the best ever amateur fighters he had something like 400 fights and only lost a handful.

I then got a part in a German war film. It was a sort of 'Hello Hello' without the laughs. It was meant to be a serious production. There I am, I'm meant to be a serious actor who's been to drama school, the lot. One of my lines was in a German accent.

"Vos is thas?" I was supposed to say. I was coming out with "Vot its has."

"No Harry, it's Vos is thas." Said the director.

"O.K. Voc it's was."

"No Harry, go again."

"Vas Vas is."

"No Harry go again."

They're now beginning to get the hump. In the end I've got a crowd of actors gathered around me, as I stand in my German SS uniform, trying to help me with the script. The scene was the German soldier kicks the door in and I come in and look around the room looking for a radio being used by a French spy. Then I find the radio equipment and hit the spy, who's in a wheelchair, with the butt of my rifle. Well, that's what was supposed to happen. It took me twenty attempts at booting the door open. When I found the radio the "vos is thas?" came out as "Vock as was?" and John, the actor in the wheelchair playing the spy, got caught in the shoulder with my rifle as I swung it too heavy handed. It was a complete fuck up. I nearly broke his bleedin shoulder! He was in agony and I swear he had tears in his eyes I don't know if they were from the pain or he was laughing at my piss poor attempt at acting.

We then do a re-take, as peoples, patience is wearing very thin "Don't hit him with the rifle," shouts the director, "when it comes to it, just grab him by the throat and we'll cut." I kick the door in, search for the radio, find it, shout "vows is its," grab him by the throat, but before the director can shout "cut" the brake on his wheelchair is off so we both go flying and knock the set down. It was more 'Some Mothers do ave em!" than Nazi Germany. Frank Spencer would have been proud of me! Everybody fell about laughing as it turned into a bit of a 'Carry on film'.

I then signed up with the top agency run by a lady by the name of Dolly Brook. I put my name down and almost straight away I got a part in 'The Bill'. Through 'The Bill' I met Mickey Monahan who used to have Euston Films. Now Micky loved his boxing and had been to a few of my shows. He was a friend of Alex Steene's and loved villains and boxers. He was the locations manager and what he said went. He had anyone he wanted on there. Anyone he didn't like never worked there again. He was the bollocks. He got me on a few episodes of 'The Bill' and gave me all the exciting bits, all the fight scenes and some great stunts. I wasn't a trained actor or stuntman. I just done it for real. I'd mixed with all the stuntmen, Tom Lucy, Greg and Nosher Powell, Steve Wilmot, Brian Nichols. I also made some great friends in Chris Elison (Burnside) Mark Wingett (Jim Carver) and Graham Cole (Stamp). They used to come to a lot of my boxing shows.

I did a scene with the actor, Graham Cole, who's still in 'The Bill' now. "Ease down a bit Harry," he said, as I grabbed him a bit too tight around the neck. As I say, I used to play it for real. I was so heavy handed. I had Graham's police radio wrapped around his neck and was nearly strangling him!

In another scene me and Greg Powell were playing bank robbers and we had to race along the road and spin the car around. Let me tell you I was shitting myself, but Greg is a more than a competent driver. In the scene I was dragged from the car by the police and shoved into the back of police van. Micky Monaghan geed the others up to go rough with me so that I'd fight back. When they played it back it looked the bollocks. There were a few bloody noses and cuts and bruises and not just on me let me tell you. There was coppers flying over the bonnet of the car, helmets up in the air, it was great fun. They left that whole scene in the episode.

My mate, Pat Prince was with me one day and the scene was that I jump up in court and have a go at the geezer in the dock. I had a jacket on with a handkerchief and a gold tie pin in the top pocket. As I jump up I lose the pin so we're all on our hands and knees looking for it. Eventually someone spotted it sticking out the geezer's head in the dock. It was hilarious!

Pat Prince also got me some good minding jobs. One was looking after Barbara Cartland, who was a lovely lady. He then had me looking after Christina Ritchie who was the pretty blonde girl in 'The Munsters' T.V. show. She was Herman and Lily's niece. She's now an even bigger star out in the States. Pat, for some reason to get me the job, had told Christina's people that I also looked after Elizabeth Taylor when she was over here. During the course of the day I had this feeling that the subject of minding Liz Taylor would pop up and sure enough, Christina's boyfriend asked me about Elizabeth. He asked what she was like, what films I'd been on with her, the lot. I knew she'd been over to this country about 6 months before doing a film so I covered my own arse and told him I'd looked after her for years except on her last visit. He seemed happy with that and dropped the subject. I then grew in confidence and told little white lies about Richard Burton and how well we got on and how we went out on the piss together. I wonder if they ever went back to Liz Taylor and told her how they'd met her English minder. "Harry who?" she would have said!

I owe an awful to Pat Prince. He's now a successful business man and good luck to him, he deserves it.

I've also worked on 'Fools and Horses' and 'Men Behaving Badly'. I've done a couple of adverts too. I done the Lynx advert with the football crowd where the geezer lets the loud horn off in me and an old girl's ear on the sidelines, and another where me and her are standing there and he lets off a red smoke flair and chokes us. I played a Welsh butcher in an advert and kept fucking up the accent, so I asked the director if we could change the lingo to a cockney accent. I was also given a part as a Brummie and spent all day and night practicing the nasal sounds of someone from Birmingham. In the end I had to admit defeat and slung myself off the job. Even the director and the producer could see the funny side. "If we ever need a cockney Harry you will be the first person we'd call."

Then my fortunes changed when I got a call from the 'Dolly Brook Agency' telling me I had a part in the BBC soap, EastEnders.

10

EASTENDERS

I got a call one morning from Dolly Brook telling me that I'd got a job as an extra on 'East Enders'. I was told to be at the Boreham Wood Studios at 8 o'clock in the morning. It's the B.B.C. studios at Elstree, Hertfordshire. I just looked at it as another job. I wouldn't say I was nervous, more excited at what lay ahead. As far as I was concerned all it was going to be was a day's work.

I turned up at the main gate, past security, parked my car and went and booked in. A runner who works at the studio came up and booked me in and ticked my name off of the list they had on a clipboard. She told me I'd be on set in half an hour so I went off and got a cuppa in the canteen which, by the way, you have to pay for. Everyone pays and no-ones treated any different. The only time you don't pay is when you're out on location.

I walked into the canteen that first morning and saw faces I recognized from the telly. Nowadays 'Holby City' is filmed in the same studios so everybody mixes. In the old days 'Kilroy' was filmed there, which I've appeared on a few times.

East Enders when I first joined was caught in the grip of the 'Dirty Den' saga (Leslie Grantham) which was exiting a time. You also had Pauline Fowler (Wendy Richard) and Pat Wicks (Pam St. Clement) who were big, big stars in the show. I done various bits and pieces in my first 6 months there, things like walking in the background in the market, or in 'The Vic' having a pint. Then I done quite a big bit, well big for me.

Where there was a boxing scene in 'The Dagmar Bar', I was seen cheering at ringside. It seems from then on my face must have fitted. The way it works is when I'm in a scene the day before filming starts I get a call from the wardrobe people saying they need me to wear such and such for such and such a scene. The assistant director, once we're kitted out on the day, will explain to us supporting artists (extras) what he or she wants us to do and where to walk, etc. When you're in a scene you have to keep quiet, and those in the background well we're miming as we chat to one another. When I have been lucky enough to get small speaking parts I realize the difference between being a supporting artist and an actor. Being an actor sounds easy and most people sit in front of their tellys at home and must think to themselves "I could do that job, its money for old rope." But believe me, it really is an art.

I recently had a scene with Shane Richie where I was selling him a Christmas tree and my line was "it will be o.k. once you let the branches settle," but what come out of my mouth was "it will be o.k. once you let the leaves settle." Well, there aint no leaves on a Christmas tree and we fell about laughing. It was so stupid; I didn't realize what I'd said. Shane Richie is a joy to work with and when he left the show I really missed him. He's a right character, a great actor who always made everyone laugh. We were filming outside in the square and a plane was going over from the local aerodrome. Straight away Shane went into the voice of the pilot flying the plane. "Just below us is the set of EastEnders where the sound of our engines will drown out their filming."

From day one I was made to feel welcome on the EastEnders set. There's an unwritten rule that you don't talk or approach any of the stars unless they talk to you. It's a thing in the film industry but to be fair I'd met quite a few of them at various boxing shows so more times than not they would come up to me and say "hello Harry, how's the boxing going?"

Boxing's a funny thing. Somewhere along the line boxers, actors, film stars, models, pop stars, villains all seem to meet somewhere along the way, and cross paths. John Bardon who plays Jim Branning in the show, when he met me, said "Harry, I'm fed up with hearing your name, now I know what you look like." John used to live in Brentford for a while and said he'd heard my name around town and in the pubs for years. John's a real down to earth fella who's done loads of things on T.V. He played alongside, comedian Jim Davidson in 'Around the Elephant and Up the Castle.' Take Barbara Windsor, a true professional who's a lovely lady. She's got time for everybody. She'll walk onto the set and chats to anyone and everyone, a real star. I have the greatest respect for that lady.

June Brown (Dot) she smokes like a trooper and also works like a trooper. She's a true pro that never forgets her lines and does all her scenes in one take. I was recently invited to her birthday party and it was a real pleasure to meet and sit with all her friends. She's been to a couple of my boxing shows. Her good friend is Rosemarie, the singer. Pam St. Clement is so nice, not the brash character Pat she plays in the show. She's a well spoken lady.

Martin Kemp of Spandau Ballet fame, now turned actor and star of 'The Krays' film about the infamous twins, was another star who was a pleasure to work with, although I'd met him before. It was a toss up between me and John H Stracey. Who showed him how to hold his hands up and box for 'The Krays ' film. John got the gig, well he was a former world champion. Martin's a lovely man and real gentleman. Mark Bannerman who played Gianni, Bepes brother (Michael Greco), is a personal friend of mine. He was one of the Italian brothers. Mark was the taller of the two, who's just had a leading part in 'Footballer's Wives.' He used to come to a lot of my boxing shows. I'm sure Mark will go on to bigger things because he's such a talented actor. Then there's my old pal, Derek Martin, (Charlie Slater) the black, cab driver and dad to the Slater posse. He drives everyone mad with his jokes. They are either very good or downright awful but we all love him. Nadia Sawalha, a lady that's left EastEnders but goes from strength to strength doing Hospital and holiday programmes, is another good friend of mine. I took her to her first ever boxing show. She was thrilled to bits by it all. She's a great crack and even put her hand in her pocket and bought a round of drinks! All the boys had the crack with her but she took it on the chin and was as good as gold.

Dean Gaffney has made the tabloid press and he's done some silly things but he's a young man and hopefully he's matured now. He's got a lovely partner, Sarah, and two lovely children. Years ago he upset one of the firm but luckily for Dean I met the fella the same day it happened and managed to square it up. Me and Dean are good pals and I've a lot of time for him.

Martine McCutcheon, she's lovely. The first day we spoke I told her that one day she was going to be a big star. She always invited me to her parties and now she is a big star. We were once filming a scene in 'The Queen Vic' and a glass bottle came off a shelf above her and hit her on the head. I told her to be careful that later she didn't suffer with concussion and gave her the name of a Doctor that I used for my boxers in Harley Street. I'm so pleased she's cracked it. I said the same thing to Tamzin Outhwaite and Kim Metcalf so really I've had a treble because they've all done well for themselves. So I must have an eye for a pretty and talented actress? But then who ain't?

Steve McFadden (Phil Mitchell) comes over as one of the boys. He's from a working class background and he knows a lot of people I know. He's a true professional and we get on well. We sometimes meet at boxing shows as Steve is a big fight fan.

One of my favourites at the moment is Kara who plays Dawn. She's a lovely looking girl, who is so warm, both on the outside and the inside; she's so caring. She has such a great personality. I think she's going to go a long, long way. I predict great things ahead for her and I can see her becoming massive in Hollywood, and don't forget you heard it from Harry Holland first.

Last, but not least, I'd like to mention Wendy Richard. Because of her dour, downbeat character in the soap people tended to take her the wrong way. I can only speak as I find but I must say I found her to be a kind, warm person. When I was ill she came across to me on the set and told me that if I ever needed to talk to somebody then I could go to her at any time. I'd been diagnosed as having prostate cancer which was in its early stages. She was so sweet.

One person I couldn't really take to was Leslie Grantham (Den Watts). He came back for a second spell on the show but I just couldn't warm to him. The problem was that years ago, whilst serving out in Germany with the armed forces, he shot and killed a cab driver. Now I know some of that cab driver's family and they described him as a hard working, loving family man who was only trying to earn a living and make a few quid. Therefore I could never really feel comfortable in Leslie Grantham's company. I never mention to him that I know his victim's family but it was always in my head whenever we spoke. I could never really 100% take to him. He wasn't my cup of tea. It really was just "hello," or "goodbye," and that was it.

In general, to be honest, it's just like being in one big family. I've now been there 20 years so I didn't do bad for what I thought was just a day's work.

Over the years I've got more and more parts in the background. After about a year I got a stall in the market, then Jonathan Ross's mum came in and got my pitch, but she's just left the show under a bit of a cloud. But speak as I find I do miss Martha Ross we had some great laughs together as with all the other stall holders who are all my muckers. I enjoyed my time working in the market and one of the funniest stories was when 'Little Britain' star, David Williams, had a small part a few years back, well before he found fame. I had an in growing toe nail which was killing me. We were filming a scene and he accidentally stepped back without looking and trod on my bad toe. Jesus, I nearly went through the roof. I felt like pushing him off but I couldn't do or say anything because "he's only a laydee." I'm just so proud to be involved in such a great show. I think I'm right in saying it's the B.B.C.s top show. I feel privileged to be a part of it as I'm a fan of the show as well.

When I'm working on set I'm like the imposter or the fan that's found himself amongst some of his favourite actors. Sometimes I feel like pinching myself. At the end of the day you drive out the gates and sometimes there's the fans waiting outside to catch some of the cast for their autographs. I feel like I should be standing out there with them. Some of the actors have done a 13 hour day, yet they've always got time to stop and sign autographs. They always have time for people.

On a normal working day there's probably between 30 to 40 supporting artists on the East Enders set. All the back ground noise you hear from the market, like, "come and get your apples, two bob a pound." "Here hurry up, all ya grapes a pound a pound." That's all added in after filming. The fruit and veg on the stalls is changed about once a week. It goes straight in the bin although we might get a banana every now and again, if you're lucky.' If you're chosen to film a scene in the café you can save your dinner money but the prop geezer always tells ya not to eat too much of it because you might end up doing half a dozen takes. The food for the café comes from the B.B.C. canteen on site. Laurie (Jane) who plays Ian Beales's girlfriend is a lovely lady and when she first started I gave her a lift to the station and we chatted, and again I forecast big things for her and fortune teller Harry was right. She's now a big part of the show. Russell Grant eat ya heart out. All the directors and production staff are very good and understanding and when it comes to a speaking part they're very patient. I've had about 10 speaking parts to date and so as Orick, who plays Winston. He seems to be coming more into it and he's done well. A few people who have helped me no-end and I have to mention them, are Troy, Wyn, Jamie, Rona McKendrick, Carolyn Weinstein, and my favourite photographer Adam Pensotti. A big thank you.

The longest period when I've not been on the show or on set 'as been sometimes weeks more than months so I count myself lucky. I now average two or three days a week, there now. That's great. My ambition on the show would be to run 'The Queen Vic' or better still, run a boxing gym or even running a pie and mash shop would do me. I look forward to the next 20 years, God willing.

When I look back at my working life I aint done too bad. I've been an apprentice on the print, I've been a van boy, and I've been a van salesman. I've delivered gin and then perfume. Then I was a bouncer and music promoter. I've run a hairdressers with the wife. Well, she run it. I didn't get involved. I wasn't light enough in me loafers to be a hairdresser. I was never going to be Harry Sasson, "COIFFEUR TO THE STARS". I've been involved at all levels with both amateur and professional boxing. I've done minding and debt collecting and have been a male escort and a male model for Marks and Spencers!

11

THE MODEL

Through a mate of mine I got a job modeling a jumper. My mate was in the film game but he supplied a few models for various jobs, for 'Marks and Spencer's I went along to their head office at Baker Street, in London and done the jumper modeling and they asked me back again.

This time I had to go to a room where there were five women sitting there in a semi circle.
" Good morning Harry, will you slip these on?" and handed me a pair of underpants. I looked around to see if they were joking. I honestly thought it was a set up for 'Candid Camera' or 'Beadles About', but they sat there all straight-faced. I realized they weren't joking and went behind a screen, stripped my own gear off and put on these Marks's Y front pants. I walked out and stood in all me glory in front of these five birds, the pants saving my blushes. I was 59 years old so I was hardly a Greek God but then again I ain't bad for an old soldier.

I'm told that they're looking for a XL size chap to model the company's underpants. That's XL all over, not just what's in the pants and I'm then told I've got the job if I want it. I was on £200 a day when I was site. I had my own office with two other blokes. It was great. At the time I was only doing one day a week on the East Enders set, so I did 3 or 4 days a week doing the underpants. When I wasn't called for I used to sit around drinking tea and coffee and reading the papers. I'd sometimes get called in to model shirts and suits but my main thing was the pants. I'd get a call a couple of hours before I was needed and then I'd go to a room and put on the underwear and these birds would measure around my ball bag area and then they'd mark off in a pen where they needed taking in or adjusting. I would then change into a similar pair, which had been washed, and they'd compare the washed to the new. It was all very scientific and a couple of times my rocket nearly went off.

When I'm fit and I go out jogging and do a bit of training I'm a 36 inch waist and if I aint been training I'm anything from a 38 to a 40 waist. Well, these designers for Marks didn't measure my waist for near on the two years I was there. So, all them poor bastards trying to squeeze into a 36 inch waist pair of pants, sorry lads it was my fault.

Whatever I modeled I got to keep. I had suits, shirts, trousers, pants, vests, tee shirts. It was all good quality gear. One of the girl models there was a right good sort and an ex page 3 girl but she'd done a bit of bird for fraud and I was the only one to know about her past. I never let on because one, I wouldn't grass on anyone and two, she had really made good for herself, and three it was none of my business. The prison sentence she done she done for other people. She was set up but fair play to her she took what she got on the chin. She was a good girl.

I used to sneak in the staff shop and have a spend up; it was so cheap in there. Marks do look after their staff well. In the end my waist was getting bigger so the job came to an end but I really enjoyed myself there. It was a joy to work there.

By now I'd stopped promoting the boxing shows and just done a bit of match making for Joey Pyle. That's when I became even closer to a lot of the villains. In my spare time I did a bit of work for my mate, Dave Evans, who's a self made millionaire who used to sell pork pies with me years ago for 'Telfers'. He started up these little plug- in air-fresheners that spray out a fresh fragrance every now and again. He used to rent them out to pubs, restaurants, shops and offices. He started them off in their early days so he made a mint out of them. He had them all over the country. Now and again people would take them for their business, use them and not pay him.

At that particular time it had gone a bit quiet on East Enders so Dave kept me busy. I was the same in this job as I was when I was bouncing. I was very polite and diplomatic and a punch up was the last resort. Talking sensibly seemed to sort a lot of the problems and debts out. I was never one to go steaming straight in, all guns blazing and shouting the odds. Being nice and calm and softly spoken did the trick.

I went into a busy pub in the heart of Brixton and I was the only white face in the whole of the pub. I approached the governor about the payments for the air freshener and he invited me down into the cellar to talk about it. He said he admired my bottle and without question he paid up.
"How about paying in advance for the next 3 months?" I asked, He handed me a wad of notes, which he'd just counted out, "don't push ya luck." He growled.

Here and there a few people would get stroppy and they'd push my patience to the limit. One particular job, like that was down at a pub in Hastings, East Sussex on the coast. It was a right shithole and nearly all the windows had been smashed in and were boarded up. It was a right state with burnt out cars in the car park. It looked more like Beruit. I walked up to the bar and asked the geezer serving if he was Mr. Smith, the landlord. "No" he said and denied being the governor. I just knew that I wasn't going to get any money out of him. He was one awkward cunt and I really was wasting my time. The next best thing to do was to get the machines out of the pub so that Dave could re-lease them again. The geezer carried on denying that he was Mr. Smith and I told him it was embarrassing knocking up such a debt on such a silly thing. He kept saying the governor wasn't in and that he couldn't help me. I now have to think on my feet and find a solution to the problem so I tell the lard arse behind the bar, some cock and bull story, that whoever installed these machines was most likely going to get the sack. I explained that he'd been ripped off over these machines, and I now had his interest and so I knew he was the governor.

"What do you mean?" he asked.

"Well, you should have never had them installed, you didn't really need them."

"Why not?"

"Well, all you had to do was kick another window in and you would have had all the fresh air you needed."

He laughed. In the end I got the machine out. I was happy, Dave was happy and the landlord was happy.

I got an hourly rate off of Dave and my travelling expenses so he looked after me well. So no matter what I recovered for him I was guaranteed my money. I used to go suited and booted and looked more like a travelling salesman than a debt collector.

A couple of times I was threatened by people who'd tell me that they were connected to villains that I personally knew. Funnily enough I visited a pub in Plumpstead, South East London, where the geezer running it told me he was good friends with Dave Courtney.

"You think you're Mr. Tough Guy?" he smiled.

"I don't think I'm Mr. Tough Guy. I'm nearly 60 years of age. I'm too old to be Mr. Tough Guy."

I told him all I was there for was to collect the money that he owed. He went on to say that he was connected to the firm.

"Well, when you see Dave Courtney tell him you've just met Harry Holland." With that he paid in full, we shook hands and I left.

A couple of funny ones were when Ray Brittle, my old mate from my amateur boxing days, asked me to help him out on a job. He explained it was a simple debt collection which we would get 200 quid each for. I didn't really want to do it but the way Ray explained it, that it was a straightforward knock on the door, cop the money and off, made it sound easy. I reluctantly agreed, but went because Ray can be very persuasive. We went to the address given to us and Ray sat in the car. I banged on the door and no one was in, so we got on the blower to the geezer we were recovering the debt for. We met up with him and got our 200 quid. He then asked us if we were interested in buying the debt off of him and that we could pay him the part of the thirty-two grand debt he was owed.

"Thirty two grand?" I said, "No-ones got that sort of money just after Christmas!"

I said I wasn't interested but as a token, because no one had been in when we called the first time, I'd go back and try again. Me and Ray drove back around there and I got out and banged on the door. The door flew open and a huge man in a string vest stood there with a growling Alsatian on a chain next to him and it was snarling and barking and chomping at the bit to stick its teeth in my arse.

"Listen you cunt," I said to the man, "put that fucking dog away. You owe thirty two grand and I want it paid."

He denied he owed the money but surprisingly put the dog back in the house and came back out, and we spoke on the doorstep. I explained to him that he had to pay the money back and that if he didn't I would be back and I wouldn't be so nice next time. I turned and walked away and we drove off. Within minutes Ray got a call on his mobile. The man on the other end was ecstatic because the bloke had agreed to pay him back on the one condition, that he didn't send that nasty man back around to his house. I even laughed at that statement myself and the geezer we collected the debt for kindly bunged us another £500 each. A nice little earner eh? What a liberty!

The word went around that I was good at my job and I was getting offers from all over the place to recover bits of lost money. On another occasion I took Andy Till with me. I don't know why I took him, I really don't as I normally like to do things my way and on my own. I told him when we get to the house, just stand there and not say a word, let me do the talking. I knocked on the door and a geezer answered.

"Mr. Jones I'm here to talk about a debt you owe."

"I don't owe no debt."

"Yes ya do."

"No I don't."

With that he's picked up the telephone in his hallway and dialed a number and asked for the police.

"I have two men standing here on my doorstep and are threatening me for money."

"No we're not."

"Yes you are."

"There's been a misunderstanding," I said, so with one ear to the phone he explains his financial position and on how he's been to the county court blah blah blah

It turns out he has been made bankrupt so it was no longer our problem. We could do nothing about recovering the money, but this fucker wouldn't let it drop. We walked up the road and this geezer still with the phone to his ear is giving the Old Bill a running commentary on where we were heading. I'm looking at Andy thinking one of us has got to whack him to get him off our case. Andy up to now to be honest hasn't said a word. With that we're stopped dead in our tracks and I've taken the phone off the bloke and in my best tones I say.

"Hello there, to whom am I speaking? There's obviously been a mistake and we'll come down to the police station straight away and sort out all this mess." I handed the geezer the phone back and now he's trying to stall for time so as the police catch us.

"If you can give me some paperwork I'll be happy to read it," says this dickhead, blatantly stalling for time. I patted him on the back and told him there had obviously been a huge mistake.

"Come on Andy my old son, let's go to the police station."

Andy looked at me.

"Andy, when we get to the top of the road run like fuck back to the car."

We fucked off a bit lively, lost the geezer and never heard any more about it.

The last one I done was for my mate, Mark Warnock who's a real steady fella, a real nice man. An Indian geezer up north had knocked him for a few bob and he asked me to help him out, and recover it. I again didn't really want to do it but he kept on so I ended up hiring a car and driving up there, with him following me in his car. He showed me the address and I knocked on the door, which turned out to be the wrong house. The geezer I wanted was a Mr. Singh who lived in the house next door. Mr. Singh came to the door and I explained he owed a certain person money. He argued that he didn't owe a penny to anyone and pushed me in the chest. He was standing in the doorway with a child about 6 years old.

"Don't be silly Mr. Singh, not in front of the child. There is a hard way or an easy way we can do this," and with that he pushes me again.

"No sir, please don't do that," and with that he comes at me again, and grabs hold of my bollocks and is squeezing as hard as he can. I had tears in my eyes and he stood looking at me with a sickly looking grin on his chops. I've grabbed him and hit him with a left hook and got his head under my arm in a headlock. He's struggling so I clumped him but he's still wanting to have a go. I run him up the hallway and put one foot on the settee and launch him and me backwards, and then he lets go. A car pulls up outside the front door with his wife in and she's witnessing what's going on. The thing is she's the one who's grassed him up about the debt and as to where we could find him. Apparently he made her life a misery and was a bit to heavy handed, so she wanted revenge. Eventually as I back off he comes at me with a lump of wood. 'Bang'! I've hit him and he's gone flying, he stumbles, around then finds his feet and runs off into a nearly mini cab office. I knew he'd gone to get help so I quickly jumped into my motor and zoomed off. Sitting at the end of the road is me mate, Mark, whose debt it was. I waved and headed towards the motorway and home. Within minutes Mark was on the blower telling me that the Old Bill had come from every direction and had swamped the place. They even had the dogs out trying to pick up my scent.

About a month later I get a phone call from the police asking if I was the driver of a hire car, registration number so and so.

"Well, there's been an assault Cambridge "

"Cambridge? I've never ever been to Cambridge. I wouldn't even know how to get there."

"Yes sir, there's been an assault."

"Assault? Assault? I'm an old age pensioner."

"Are you?"

"Yes, I am also an actor. You often see me in a well known T.V. soap. I'm the old boy who sits in the corner, who walks with the aid of a walking stick."

"I'm so sorry sir, there seems to have been some mistake. Sometimes the C.C.T.V. cameras pick up car registrations wrongly. You'll hear no more about this sir."

He then apologized again and that was that. I did get another call on the matter a few weeks later but again I played dumb and heard no more.

That was me retired from debt collecting. I was now 60 and I don't think the old ticker could cope with all the shit and stress. After a hard days work recovering money. I used to like to go out and relax and have a few beers. One night I ended up in "Stringfellows." I knew Peter personally and I was the butt of one of his practical jokes, which nearly got me and a mate killed. Me and me mate went out to Miami on holiday and Peter recommended we stay at this hotel that he knew. He gave us all the old bollocks, and it sounded really nice. But in fact when we got there it was in a seedy run down part of town. Anyway, some locals with guns, who unbeknown to us were just about to pull up next to us and rob us, followed us in a car. What we didn't know was that the police had been watching all this and stepped in and arrested these blokes. So I'm in "Stringfellows" this night and I get chatting to a couple at the bar. They seem very nice and she goes off onto the dance floor and him and me carry on talking. He then tells me that his wife likes me, and that she fancies a sandwich. I tell him that there's a restaurant upstairs and I'm sure they'll do her what she likes." What does she like egg and tomato or cheese and pickle?" No Harry, your misunderstanding me the sandwich she fancies is lying down into between you and me. I nearly spat me drink out all over him. She wasn't a half- bad sort. Next thing, she disappears off of the dance floor and comes back and hands him her knickers which he stuffs in his pocket. " We've spoke about having a threesome with another fella for years. But we've never found someone we both like. That is until tonight." She came back off the dance floor and grabbed me and rubbed herself up and down as we boogied. Fuckin hell it was heaven. The sad thing was she got so pissed the husband ended up carrying her out. So that was the end of the threesome. I did bump into them when I was at 'Olympia' for the annual 'Erotica' show. And they were demonstrating a 'Shagging' chair, the husband had invented, which you could have sex in while it hung from the ceiling. I did have a quick word with them but they were so busy, they didn't seem to take a lot of notice.

12

THE STUD

One day I get a call from a mate of mine who ran an escort agency. He was in need of a male escort to keep a lady company who was on his books. You know the sort of things, go out to dinner, or the theatre or the ballet, all the things I just love. The thing is I tend to go for birds a lot younger than me simply because I'm young at heart and a bit of a Peter Pan. I'm the original boy who didn't and couldn't grow older. I'm still like that to this day.

The lady I've been asked to take out turns out to be 50 so I thought it was another wind up, but what did I have to lose? In my own way I've always seen myself as a bit of a ladies' man. I've always been a bit tongue in cheek and had that a bit of devilment in me more than anyone else.

Anyway, I'm given her home phone number so I give her a bell. She tells me her name's Pauline and she tells me a little bit about herself and then tells me that if I am to be her escort she doesn't wish to have sex. I just wish to go out and have a pleasant evening. I'm still thinking it's got to be a wind up so I say "that's all right love, we'll do what ever you fancy." She gives me her address in Barnes, which if you don't know is a right nice area. So off I go. I'm suited and booted and arrive at the house and what a drum, it's got to be a million pound plus, easily. I ring the doorbell and the front door opens. Standing there is a rather attractive woman in a negligee. I can tell straight away she must have been a good sort in her time and to tell ya the truth she was worth a shot now.

"Are you Harry?"

"Yes."

"Are you Pauline?"

"Yes."

"I like the look of you Harry," she purrs and she invites me in. Now I know it aint a wind up. I follow her through into the lounge and the brain in my head and the main brain inside my trousers kick into action.

"I think Harry darling," she says almost in a sexy whisper "it's too late to go out tonight so would you care to join me in a glass of wine?"

"Certainly, but I must tell you Pauline that I will be having to make tracks pretty soon."

To tell ya the truth I was a big worried about shagging her. Well, not worried about the act of shagging her it was just when I made love I couldn't do it wearing protection. I know I can hear you saying it's on a plate you divvy prat but the problem was if she used male escorts regularly how many blokes had hung out of the back of her. Call me old fashioned but I wasn't going to get myself riddled with some sex disease or aids. Fuck that.

"Now don't get me wrong Harry darling. I insist on paying you."

"Well love," I said trying to hide the lump in my bulging trousers, "its 100 quid for the first hour and 100 quid for every half an hour after that."

"But Harry darling I like to haggle," and she pouted her lips and pushed her breasts out. I'm now a muttering, stammering wreck who's nearly coming in his pants (Marks & Spencers). It went all quiet.

"Harry I really like you but you're a saucy bastard," she said. I nudged her and laughed and said half jokingly "well give us four hundred quid and we'll call it quits." I'm really trying to get out now because she aint going to give me £400 for nothing.

"Pauline," I said, "you said over the phone that you didn't even want sex."

"A lady is allowed to change her mind, Harry darling."

"Pauline dear, I haven't come prepared, do you understand me?" I explained I had no durex and to cut a long story short she got half-pissed and I copped the 400 quid, and we had a nice drink and from that night on we became good friends. It turns out her husband had died and left her a lot of money and months later she gave me some of his old clobber, including a lovely Crombie overcoat. I gave it to my mate. As I already had one. I didn't mind slipping into a dead mans woman, but not coats. I never did shag her but she was a good, fit sort.

One evening I turned up there and she was laid out on the floor pissed. She obviously had a bit of a drink problem. I stripped her and put her to bed and the next day she phoned to apologise.
"Did anything happen between me and you last night?" she asked.
I put her mind at rest but I was half tempted to kid her along just to see what reaction I would have got. She was a good woman and if you're still out there Pauline I hope you're well darling.

My mate at the agency was well pleased. He was expecting 10% of 100 quid and he ended up getting a cut from the £400. He later called me again to go on another date and I was going to say no but the curiosity got the better of me. It turns out that this bird was only 30, well within my age bracket. She lived over in Ealing, West London. I got to the address and this dolly bird answers the door straight away, and I fancy it.
   "Harry?"
   "Yes."
   "Oh."
   "You look surprised."
   "Well normally I have someone a bit younger."
   "Would you like me to go?"
   "No, you seem nice, come in for a drink."
   She introduced herself as Gwen and I went in and had a drink. She put on some slow smoochy music on and we had a cheek to cheek dance. It's turning out to be a right crack and this is looking brand new when suddenly the doorbell goes. She turns the music down and goes and opens the front door.
   "Hello darling, do come in," and I can hear the sound of lips

smacking. "Who the fuck's this?" I'm thinking. I sit down not having a clue to what is going on, when in comes this right good looking geezer, he's like a male model, he shakes my hand. She's now stumbling about pissed and puts the music back on. He's looking at me and I'm looking at him as for a clue to what's going on. She fucks off over the other side of the room and sorts out some drinks.

"You an escort mate?" he asks.

"Yeah."

"Don't worry so am I and I've been here before."

He asked the bird what was going on as there was three of us and he felt a bit awkward.

"There's 3 things we can do. Either Harry goes and I stay or I go and Harry stays, or we both stay and have a good time."

Fuck you mate, you aint coming nowhere near me," I'm thinking, "count me out." No way was he getting stuck up me if that was what he was implying. She totters to her handbag and takes out a wad of notes and counts out £110 and hands it to me. She then tells the other bloke to go. I'll always remember his face, he went white.

"Are you sure?" he asked.

"I know what I'm doing."

"Are you sure?"

"Just go," she says and with that he headed for the front door.

"I'll see ya out mate," I said, following him up the hallway.

"Sorry about that mate," I said as I shook his hand, as we stood on the doorstep.

"Don't worry about it; it's the way it goes."

"Here, cop a tenner for ya petrol," and I handed him a cockle. I really fancied this bird; she was a right sort, so I'd had a right result. I took her upstairs to her bedroom and we did the lot well we nearly did the lot we stopped at having have full sex. We were both bollock naked and then she crashed out in my arms. I'm lying flat on me back with her wrapped around me and every now and again I check my watch. I gave her an hour then I half sort of woke her up out of her drunken stupor. I told her that if I stayed it would cost her more money. She didn't reply but just laid there in a deep, deep sleep, snoring her head off.

I never heard from her again and I really wanted to ring her but I didn't. To be fair I was 60 years old and she was 30, so I'd be kidding myself if I thought she'd fancied me. Here I was, 60, just retired from debt collecting and now it was time to turn it in as a paid stud.

13

THE MASONS

In 1987 I became a Freemason. The whole thing about the Masons impressed me. I'd been to dos and Ladies Nights at various lodges and I just liked the feel of the whole set up. A fella I knew, a Mr. Shaw, always spoke so enthusiastically about being a Mason and I suppose he was the one that initially got me interested.

I was initiated after an interview. It's no secret as to what goes on. You're seen, and then you're voted in. Yet we're still called a secret society. Our head office is in Covent Garden, Central London, and at the temple there is a museum, which is a really interesting place to visit. You can read up on the history of Freemasonry and what we are actually all about. There are certain things and rituals, which we don't talk about, but some people misunderstand us. We are not a sinister society. Freemasonry is all about helping each other.

We do a lot of charity work and raise lots of money for worthy causes. We don't talk about it or brag about it, but we do work for good causes. The good thing about Freemasonry is that its open to all colours, all religions, its politic free and everyone's welcome. There's no devil worshipping or cutting of throats and setting fire to witches. It's a place where sensible, like-minded people gather to socialize and mingle. It's as simple as that.

Sometimes you get invited to other lodges where you can meet nice and interesting people you wouldn't get to meet at your own lodge. Through the Masons I met a fella named Frank O'Neil who was the official photographer for the Irish Guards. He invited me to a function and what I never knew until I got there, was that the Queen Mother was taking the salute from the Irish Guards. Frank asked me if I'd like to join in the ranks on the parade. Everywhere I looked there were geezers with all sorts of medals hanging from their chests. It was embarrassing. I didn't even have a Blue Peter badge to wear. Anyway, I followed along at the tail end and when it come to taking the salute from the Queen Mum I did bottle out and slipped into the crowds. Afterwards I thanked Frank for inviting me and was going to shoot off.

"Hold up Harry," said Frank, "we've got the do now at St. James Palace."

To cut a long story short we go off to St. James Palace. All the veterans are out in their medals, and the Guards with their red tunics and bear skin Busbys, stand to attention on the steps. It's a lovely sunny day as the Queen Mum comes out and down the steps and gives all of them a piece of shamrock. The band played "When Irish eyes are smiling". It was a beautiful day and the Queen Mum looked radiant. A couple of fellas came over who recognized me from the boxing so we stood on the steps and I had my photo done with them. We then had another done next to the sentry and while we're chatting away the Queen Mother re-appears and is standing talking to people in a line. The thing is I'd taken with me a plastic Lidyl shopping bag to keep my bits and pieces in. I put that down out the way behind the sentry box and quickly joined the queue. I said to the woman in front of me.

"How does one address the Queen Mum?"

"You say your majesty and then bow." She said. In no time at all I was in front of her. I bowed.

"Pleased to meet you your majesty."

"And you," came her reply. Standing next to her was a geezer suited and booted who informed Her Majesty who it was she was meeting. He looked at me blankly and before he could say anything I was off. Good job I still didn't have me Lidyl's bag as the old girl might have thought I was a contestant on 'Ready Steady Cook' and was about to knock her up a tuna bake with sweet potatoes and a rocket salad! That would have been hilarious if I'd tipped the contents of me bag out and told her I'd spent £4- 44p. I did manage to get a photo of me standing in the grounds with the Queen Mum in the background, just over my shoulder. So I've met some lovely people through the Masons and had some lovely nights. I've had some funny moments as well.

A fella I know who's a bit deaf was sitting in a meeting with an Indian fella. Now this Indian bloke had an accent straight out of one of those 70s sitcoms like 'Mind Your Language' or 'Love Thy Neighbour'. Every time the Indian geezer spoke the deaf fella could hardly hear him and his strong accent didn't help.

"What's he saying?" he asked, looking around the room.

"What? What?"

We were all trying not to laugh, it was so funny. There was blokes holding their stomachs and had tears in their eyes trying to stifle the laughter. Even the old boys who'd been in the lodge for years found it amusing. At one point even the Indian geezer raised his eyes to the heavens and chuckled. Masons being racists is complete cobblers and something like that just shows it. We are one big family regardless of the colour of someone's skin.

Five years ago I met Prince Michael of Kent and I was so proud to have met him. In history there's been some very famous people associated with the Masons you've had the likes of Winston Churchill, Shackleton, Lord Nelson, George Washington, John Wayne, Robbie Burns, and many others. Since I've joined I've become Master of the Lodge, and two years ago I was made 'A Grand Officer' in the near future I hope to go even higher. One thing's, for sure I'm so proud to be a part and to be involved in Masonry.

14

JOEY PYLE

I've known Joe for years from my amateur boxing days. Joe had something to do with 'The Rosehill Boxing Club' and used to have the 'Carshalton Arms' pub, in the same area. From then on we became friends. He used to be good friends with Johnny Cheshire, the ex boxer. He used to like the way my boys from the Hogarth Club fought. I've got the greatest respect for Joe. He's a lovely, lovely man. I've worked as a matchmaker for Joe's son, Joe Junior.

One day we were having a bit of a disagreement over something or other and I was getting the hump and had to raise my voice to get my point of view across. Joe was sitting there.
"Cor blimey," he said, "is he always like this?" and we had a good laugh at my outburst. Joe himself was a good amateur boxer and I've seen him take young Joe on the pads. Joe's best mate was the late Alex Steene. As I say I'd worked with his son Greg and between us we done 16 shows in one year. A lot of work goes into putting a show on. I was managing, promoting, matchmaking, it was unbelievable the amount of work I put in to make a success of these shows. John Bloomfield took a lot of weight off of me. He'd train the boys and on fight night he'd get the boys warmed up, do some pad work and bandage their hands and get them gloved up.

The thing with John was he'd panic over certain things which would only be silly little things. One day we were getting Garry Hobbs ready to go in the ring and John, bless him, was giving Gary a bit of a pep talk, but it was all going terribly wrong.

Ray Winstone, who is not only a top actor but was a top class amateur boxer

Chris Elison from 'The Bill' (Burnside)

Me, Joey Pyle and April

Me, Daniella, April and Michael

The 'Rockers' at Wimbledon Station. Motor bikes frighten the life out of me, but I daren't tell nutty Dave

The gang from Tenerife

Shakin Stevens talking about old times

Jeff Johnson who's been a great friend since I was 5 years old, with Bubbs Plummer

Modelling at Marks, the geezer in the picture is how I used to look

With Mark Warnock at 'The Lodge'

Here I'm going to surprise a lot of people by revealing that I was once a prison officer. Not really, I'm on the set of 'Midsummer Murders', so put down ya phones, I ain't a wrongen

In Vagas for the Lennox Lewis v David Tutu fight. Here I'm with a couple of the local fellas

My John with barry Jones ex-Super Feather Weight World W.B.O. and I.B.F. champion. John now trains Barry

"You want to watch this geezer Gary, he can bang. He's a big puncher. He fought Earl Edwards and he smashed Earl down and all around the ring."

Gary Hobbs is now shitting himself and is a bundle of nerves.

"Hang on John," I said "who won that fight?"

"Earl Edwards," he replied. He'd got all mixed up and instead of building Hobbs's confidence up he got his talk arse about face and just confused the issue. I think John was more nervous than Gary, but that was John for ya. He had some funny sayings too. Say the ref was to pull one of our fighters up for slapping or hitting with the inside of the glove, John would poke his head through the ropes and shout,

"You wouldn't like to take it off of him ref."

Another one of his was "everything comes off of the job." I'd like a pound for every time he said that. That was his favourite.

Him and me were out one night in 'Rockys Bar' in Twickenham when a geezer started getting a bit lairy. John's put one on his chin and half knocked the geezer out. John was a big, strong man who could look after himself. I've got one leg and John's got the other and we've slung this geezer out the back. Half an hour later we're talking to the bouncer on the front door and this pisshead that John's clumped earlier has re-appeared, all groggy and asking us if we'd seen anybody hit him. "No mate, we've just got here," we both said.

Alex Steene was a great character and was Joey Pyle's right hand man. Alex could be found ringside at most boxing shows wearing his trademark dark glasses. You may have spotted him on T.V. sitting with Frank Warren and the like. The glasses made him look like a gangster but he wore them not as a fashion accessory but because of his bad eyes. He had the biggest shoulders you've ever seen and looked a very powerful man, both in physique and presence. Me. Alex, Joe and John Conteh were all walking along the road going to the Bruno- Witherspoon fight at Wembley stadium, and as we walked past this group of young fellas one of them said, "Who does that geezer in the dark glasses think he is, a gangster?" "If only you knew," I thought to myself.

Since Alex sadly passed away I really do miss him. He was a great, great character. Through Alex I met Eddie Richardson, brother of Charlie. I also met the Nashs who've been well known around London for many years and are a well respected family. Alex used to run a ticket agency just off Trafalgar Square. He always had a story to tell. I used to go up and see Greg and we'd be chatting about something to do with the boxing and Alex would come in and tell us a funny story or he'd say he'd heard from Ronnie or Reggie and that they sent their love. He'd sometimes come in with a bar of chocolate and offer to share it with us. Me and Greg would be trying to do business and his dad would be bored and try to relieve his boredom with a joke or two.

Every year Alex and his lovely wife, Anna, would go to 'The Variety Royal Performance'. You'd have the Queen in the royal box and above or next door would be Alex sitting in his trademark dark glasses. Through Joe I met Freddie Foreman and his son, Jamie, who is a now an established actor in his own right and was once married in real life to the actress who played Martine McCucheon's mum in EastEnders. So there's the connection. Freddie, in the 60s, was a very close friend to the Kray twins and he's a well-respected man in his own right. I first met John Conteh when he was training at 'The Café Royal' for one of his world title fights, in them days before we became mates he was a hero of mine. He was as good as everyone said. His down fall was his brother getting involved in his boxing affairs and sort of giving him the wrong advice. He suffered with a bit of hand trouble in a couple of his fights and at one of his fights he opened up a massive gash above his opponents eye and this geezers corner must have stuffed it with what looked like cement. I've never seen anything like it. The stuff was like yellow concrete and fuck knows how they got away with that. If I remember rightly the last two fighters Conteh fought both had women's names, which were Ivy Brown and Jesse Burnett. John came along to a few of my promotions with Greg Steene at the 'Porchester Hall' in the front row was Tommy Farr, Charlie Magri, John Conteh, and Alan Minter, it was a top turn out for what was only a small show. Johns a smashing fella who's done a lot for British boxing. Most boxers away from the ring are nice fellas. John H Stracey who I mentioned before was a prime example, he had a heart of gold and his other talent was as a singer. John's got a great voice and I've been to watch him at my mate Wally Angliss's place in Twickenham. He also got together with John Burton and done some shows at 'The Britannia' in Docklands.

Roy Dennis is another good friend of mine who owns three pubs around the Fulham area. He was with John Bindon the night he stabbed and killed John Darke at a club in Putney. Roy could have a row and didn't suffer fools gladly.

At one of my shows one night a drunk geezer was cutting up rough and was being a pest. Before I could chuck him out Roy had hooked him and the fight carried on out into the hotel car park. I managed to get Roy and a few of the boys into a mini bus and away. As I'm standing there with cuts and bruises and me shirt ripped open I could hear the police sirens heading my way. "What the fuck am I doing here?" I'm thinking to myself, and I shot into one of the rooms. We used to have a lot of the Rocky Kelly weigh-ins at one of Roy's pubs.

I've met Frankie Frazier a few times and had obviously heard of his name and his reputation from years back. When I was a young man in the West End Frankie's name would often crop up as someone not to mess with.

Lenny McLean was a man I met years ago who, at the time, only weighed about 14 stone. We got chatting and we both discovered we done door work. Lenny explained to me how he dealt with any trouble and he said anyone in the vicinity of him when it was going off would get battered with a pickaxe handle. When he fought Roy Shaw at The Rainbow Theatre in Finsbury Park, North London, Frank Warren put the show on with Joey Pyle.

A lot of these boys came over to a 'Ladies' Night' at my lodge one evening and to be honest I wasn't too sure how it would go. As in most lodges there's a fair quota of policemen and anyone will tell ya that socially most villains and policemen don't mix in the same circles. Well, some do for obvious reasons but most don't. Through both sides' jobs they know who's who. Frankie Frazier and Dave Courtney was there. When I made my entrance as Worshipful Master you are slow hand clapped in. I was told later that Roy Shaw wasn't sure what to do so as well as clapping he shouted out "yeah," at the top of his voice. He'd asked Joey Pyle what the evening was all about before they got there. But Joe was none the wiser and couldn't give him an answer. Johnny Allen from EastEnders came along but the boys hadn't exactly explained what sort of night they were going to so he came over in a normal suit and tie and us lot were all in dinner suits. It was a great night and to top it all, Sean Williamson, Barry from East Enders, sang the Ladies' song for me and believe me that fella can really sing. He's got a terrific voice. It's a song dedicated to all the ladies present for being understanding and letting their men out. It's then a toast to the ladies and everyone raises their glasses to them.

You can imagine the whole thing. There's the police with many high ranking officers, the villains, the actors, the ladies. It was one night I will never forget. I got as pissed as a parrot. The food, the company, the whole lot was good. Dave Courtney was on top form that night and had us all in stitches.

I remember watching Dave box when he was a kid. I saw him do a little exhibition spar years ago with Nigel Benn and he didn't look half bad. Dave said to me years ago, "Harry, I don't know why you don't do a book." He said he'd done his books on villains and villainy but he said by the sounds of it my story had got the lot, the boxing, the acting, the birds, the villains, and the music. It would be a great read. He really encouraged me to sit down and put pen to paper.

Getting back to Dave, as a boxer let me tell ya if I'd have had him as a kid and had trained him and he had knuckled down, he would have been a champion. Dave never takes himself too seriously, but there's a lot of jealousy towards Dave from some quarters. He admits he's not the big villain he's portrayed to be. He respects the Freddie Formans and the Joey Pyles of this world. I've heard it from his own mouth. He loves the limelight and he loves the crack. He's what I would call a celebrity gangster but he's good at what he does. In no uncertain terms is he a weak man, he's far from it. He's clever and that's his strength. He can tell a good tale and he's a nice man. I have the utmost respect for him. The thing is a lot of what he writes in his books is the truth and some people don't like the truth. When he says that some of the old faces are getting on a bit and living in the past and that nowadays these new breed of youngsters don't give a fuck, well, he's telling the truth. It's as simple as that. Respect has gone out of the window. What chance have you got against a younger fella if you don't keep yourself in shape? Nowadays reputations count for fuck all. Some of them would shoot ya as quick as look at ya. It's a whole new ball game, a different culture. I hear of kids as young as 10 and 11 carrying guns. Yeah, I had a gun at 10 but it was plastic and fired bits of potato.

It's funny how you get a real cross section of people who like boxing. On the East Enders set I was given the job of teaching the actress Daniella Westbrooke how to box. She had a fight scene with Bianca, Patsy Palmer, and she picked it up very quickly. She looked good when she was shadow boxing. Patsy Palmer's dad and her had something to do with a gym, down at Bethnal Green Road. One of my old fighters, Terry Butwell, used to train there when it was called the 'Bulldog gym'. Terry had won 5 world championships as a kick boxer and when I first got him I thought I'd discovered a real gem. He had 5 fights with me but only won 2. He was a great kid but as a pro boxer he lacked something. In my gym at the time I had some quality boxers so he was a small fish in a big pond.

John Bardan, who plays Jim Branning, had to fight Ron Moody of 'Oliver' fame. I had to show Jim how to bandage his hands up, but it was great working with the two of them. I've also stunt co-ordinated a fight scene in 'Footballers' Wives' which was a crack. I played the referee in the ring at an unlicenced fight. It was my idea for one bloke to nut the other as the bell went. The director loved it and we filmed it the way I had suggested it. I got the Lynx advert through someone seeing me on that episode of 'Footballers' Wives'.

The Lynx advert was filmed on some playing fields over in Hendon, North London. We filmed about 3 or 4 of them all in the same day. Originally there was about 20 of us lined up and the casting director went along the line. I had my trademark gold boxing gloves hanging from a chain and I could sense him keep looking at them. He was almost hypnotized by them. I had a funny feeling I was going to get the job and I did. It was a great advert and the kid who played the lead is a proper actor who is good at his job.

I done silent Witness for TV. And I got Charlie Magri and Terry Marsh a part. I had my son, John, playing a trainer. The lead actress, Amanda Burton asked me if I'd introduce her to Terry, as she was a big fan of his. She's a lovely looking lady and as soon as I could I called Terry over and he came over as quick as a shot. Brian Nichols, who fought my son John 3 times as an amateur, is now a successful stuntman. He was Andy Till's stable mate. Brian worked on 'Footballers' Wives' with me. I also used to work with Derek Lee who does all the Bond films. I taught him how to box. Denise Rine who's a stuntwoman and a good friend and great at her job has put my name up for loads of work, which I've been lucky enough to get.

I have the greatest admiration for all the stuntmen and women I've worked with and I think sometimes what they do goes unnoticed. They should get more credit for the great job that they do.

15

MADELINE
(Bad mistake?)

Over the last few years my involvement in boxing 'as wound down but my career in EastEnders had picked up. I was now working more days there and the show has taken over more of my life. Johnny Bloomfield started helping out at another gym with Jim Evans and was training Geoff McCreesh. So I started to wind my stable down. I wanted to concentrate more on my acting career, which I'd been doing. But for the last five years I've been keeping my hand in with the boxing as a matchmaker for all the major promoters. I've worked for Joey Pyle, Bruce Baker, Jess Harding, John Fald, and Audley Harrison. In fact Audley wanted me at one time to be his promoter but my licence had run out at the time and I didn't realize it. I did renew it but I then let it lapse again. The rules state that I should have promoted two shows before I could then go on and promote a championship fight.

I now work in Audley's corner as his cut's man. I've done 3 or 4 fights with Audley and I'll tell ya what, he's an absolute gentleman. He's nothing like some people think of him. You have to have arrogance to be a good fighter. Sometimes what he says is taken the wrong way and at times he's misunderstood. He's very confident, he's got the skill, the bottle and guts to go all the way to the top.

He beat Danny Williams in a re-match so the world's his lobster now. When he put his shots together he's a world beater. He's got a fantastic jab. After the first Williams fight the dressing room was like a morgue. We were all gutted. As I came out of the hall I felt choked for him. I didn't want to go out on the booze; I just wanted to get home. I felt choked for his manager, Hazel. She puts so much hard work in but when he won the re-match it was party time. But that's the highs and lows of boxing. If he ever did win a World Title I think he'd hold on to the title for a long time. He'd make a great world champion both inside and outside of the ring. He's very articulate and can hold himself up well. He reminds me very much of Lennox Lewis.

I saw Lennox's first pro fight and I was there at Audley's, and after seeing both of their first few fights I'd say that Audley would be just a shade in front of Lennox. But we will have to wait and see if he rises to the top as Lennox did. Lennox came on a bundle after he won the Title and I feel Audley could do the same. Both Lennox and Danny Williams had fought the once great Mike Tyson and beaten him, but did they both fight the real Mike Tyson? He was past his sell by date and to me he would have beaten both of them one after the other on the same bill on the same night if it had been in his hay day. I'd have loved to of had a Mike Tyson. He was right up my alley. He was my kind of fighter. I look at a lot of heavyweights and to me most of them are lazy. You have the exceptions like Tyson and Evander Hollyfield, but they are the exceptions.

I'm 65 this year and I still run 3 or 4 times a week. I also swim a mile a couple of times a week down the local baths. Eighteen months ago I was diagnosed as having prostrate cancer which was caught in its early stages. It could come to surgery but as I write I'm holding it off from having an operation. The reason being there's so many horrible side effects. The doctors would like to remove the prostate but that could affect my everyday life. I would be impotent straight away. I may also need a colostomy bag and I'm too vain for that. I know a few people who had the op and they wished they hadn't. There's a team that look after me at Ashford Hospital and another at Guildford. Doctor Paine, a lady doctor who I know really well, understands me and has been brilliant. I've told her I love a young bird and that I need everything in good working order. She laughs at me and says "Mr. Holland, most people that come to see me ask am I going to live? Your first question was, will I still be able to get an erection?!"

I'm now divorced, which was totally down to me. My John had his jaw broken in a fight and I met the girl who'd helped him. Her name was Madeline and she was 19. She was a real stunner, drop dead gorgeous and had the most beautiful smile. I couldn't get her out of my mind from our first meeting. I was 46 and should have known better. We got chatting and I offered her a job at one of my shows as a board girl which if you don't know is the girl who gets in the ring in between rounds skimpily dressed and holding up the round number. Usually the crowd cheer, jeer and wolf whistle with the usual chorus of "get your tits out for the lads." It's all showbiz because if it's on T.V. they and all their friends get to see it, plus they cop 50 quid for their 15 minutes of fame. She came from the Beavers Estate in Hounslow near my old mate, Johnny Bloomfield. He once asked me how I was getting on with the bird and I replied "that when I kissed her I knew I was in love."

"Shut up ya dopey prat," was his caring reply.

At the time she was living at home with her mum and her step dad. She had no boyfriend so she came and done the board girl job for me. One thing led to another and I arranged to take her out for a drink and then it just went from there as my feelings got stronger and stronger. Some people at the time thought that I was leading this young girl astray but they didn't know what they were talking about. She was on the pill at 14. Yes, I was older but I'm sick of being portrayed as the villain of the piece. She was never Miss Innocent. I treated her with respect and I wined and dined her and took her out on some lovely dates. I didn't hear her complaining.

Her mum used to work with a friend of mine. She used to brag to my friend Shirley how lovely I was, and how well I looked after her daughter. But she was a hypocrite because one night Madaline didn't want to leave me but we managed to pull ourselves apart and when she went indoors her mum's at home with some friends.

"Where you been with that Harry Holland?" her mum asked her, half showing off and name dropping in front of the company.

Madeline's reply was "so what? I love him." Next minute I get the call that her mum wants to see me.

The next day I went round there to see her and the mum got a bit nervous and drove away from the house without speaking to me. Eventually we sat down with one another. She told me in no uncertain terms that because of the age difference the relationship should stop. I replied that the only person who could pull the plug on it was Madeline. I told her I wasn't going to disappear or run away because she disapproved of our relationship. It wasn't going to happen, not in a million years. She told me that maybe Madeline saw me as some kind of Sugar Daddy and that I saw her as some kind of gangster's moll. Yes, at the time I was in the limelight and was well known, but to me this was real love and I was in love with this girl and age for me didn't come into it.

The thing that bought it to a head was one night me and her went out with Frank Maloney and his wife down in Kent. I ended up staying at Frank's pub with her all night so when I got home I knew there'd be murders. The first person at home I saw was my daughter Tracey. I sat her down and told her I was in love with someone else. "Its Madeline ain't it?" she asked, and I replied "yes,"

"I just knew it." She said angrily.

This all happened just before Christmas, 1987. I then had to sit my wife Jan down and tell her and you can imagine what she said. I don't think she suspected that I was playing away and didn't really see it coming. She was a good woman who I'd been married to for 24 years. But things just weren't right. For a period she'd had a bit of a drink problem, maybe bought on by me? Who knows? But I'm pleased to say now it is under control, but I was the bastard in our relationship. I was the jealous one and was very possessive. She was a lovely looking woman and if anyone dared to look at her, I'd go mad. She did ask me to stay for that Christmas for the sake of the kids and I did agree, but that all changed when about a week before Christmas we got a card through the front door and in it it told Jan that I was carrying on with a young girl half my age from the Beavers Estate. That was it, the final nail in the coffin. My marriage was over. She told me it was best that I went there and then as she felt as if everybody was talking about her. She was drained. This whole thing had taken its toll. I looked at her and she was no longer the sexy woman I'd loved and had cherished for all those years. I'd broken her heart but I knew I couldn't give Madeline up. Even if I'd have wanted to it was too late now. There was no turning back.

What I should have done in hindsight was to have sorted my finances out and where to stay before I left, but for some reason I'd done nothing. That night I phoned Madeline and asked her if she still wanted to be with me. "Yes," she replied, and she packed a small bag and I picked her up at the end of her road. We headed off to 'The Heathrow Park Hotel' where I'd staged a lot of my boxing shows. I done a deal with the fella there and I stayed there for 3 months. While we were staying there a solicitor knocked on the door one day and served the divorce papers on me. We then moved to Beech Road in Bedfont and then that's when things started to go wrong. What happened was Jan froze my money. Madeline's mum was pulling against me and filling Madeline's head with shit like asking why we couldn't buy our own place and why was it I could no longer afford to take her out to nice places any more? Then for a while things began to improve. We went out to Tenerife for my birthday and my mate on the day set off a big firework display. It was a fantastic time and the spark came back in our relationship but sadly towards the end of the holiday the bickering started up again and we rowed about our finances and where was all my money? Before we'd come away she'd been supporting the pair of us. She'd bring her wage packet home from work every week unopened and then we'd have a divvy up on what was to be paid and what wasn't. It was as bad as that. She had a job at the Western International Market over near Southall in the offices. I hated her working there. I was so jealous. I hated her working with all them blokes sniffing around her. I was just so jealous I don't know how Jan put up with it for all those years. We had so many rows about blokes talking to her or looking at her. I've even locked her indoors. How sad was that? I was one horrible bastard.

One day me and me Jeff mate were going off scuba diving in my white convertible and as we drove along the road we passed Jan heading for the laundry, pushing a pram full of washing with the three kids running along side her.

"Are you going to stop and help her?" asked me mate.

"No, she likes a bit of exercise," I laughed. But I was serious.

The Madaline saga came to an end and what didn't help matters was my youngest daughter Tracey trying to pull her out of my car as we sat at a set of traffic lights. She was with her boyfriend at the time, Paul. I shouted to Paul to get hold of her but he froze as he didn't know what to do. I managed to release Tracey's grip and we drove off. I felt a bit awkward. I was torn between making sure that Madeline was all right but in the same token I hated leaving Tracey there in a temper and upset at the sight of her own dad with a girl as young as her.

That night and the following morning she didn't really say a lot so that night as usual I went off to the gym with Johnny Bloomfield. I came home to find she'd fucked off with most of her gear. I spoke to her mum who came on the phone and told me she was so upset it was best left that I speak to her the next day. When I did eventually speak to her she told me the incident, since it had happened with Tracey, had really upset her and played on her mind. She said she didn't realize just how much she'd upset my family. We spoke on the phone every day that week and one day I could hear her stepfather, who she never particularly got on with, trying to grab the phone off of her and put it down. I could hear there was a lot of struggling going on and a lot of "tell him to fuck off and leave you alone." In the end she re-packed her bags and came back to me.

We were happy for a while but her mum kept interfering and poking her oar in. In the end it done my nut in and I'm wondering what the fuck I'd done. I love my kids and I was putting them through all this shit. I'd fucked everything up and I was putting the whole family through hell. The only way to try to put things right was to get rid of Madeline so in my mind, the next time we had a row, she was going to go. In my brain I had it worked out that she'd go back to her mother's and I would go back to Jan.

This day we'd gone and had a steak at the 'Duke of York' Steakhouse where my John's girlfriend, Darcey used to work. We started arguing in there and she walked out. My plan was going to plan. I said to John's missus to be, "don't worry she's going today," as she looked at me a bit puzzled. I followed Madeline out, picked her up further along the road in the car and stopped at a shop and bought a pack of black bin liners. "What they for?" she enquired. "We've run out of rubbish bags for the bin at home," I said and she ignored me. We never spoke all the way home. I went through the front door, up the stairs, opened her wardrobe and drawers and threw all her belongings into the plastic sacks. She stood there crying. I told her she had pushed me too far and now we were history.

I loaded her and her gear up in the car where there's floods of tears. "You can't do this to me Harry," she sobbed. The thing was I didn't have a clue what to do with her that was the problem. She'd fallen out with her mum over me so she couldn't go home. I was in a right temper and drove around for ages in a trance. The more she cried and moaned the angrier I got. This girl had fucked my head up and for that moment in time I hated her. Then I got the bright idea to drop her and her gear outside 'The Beavers' pub on the estate. I walked in and dropped her gear on the floor. The few people in there looked to see what was going on. "Madaline's home everybody," I shouted, and turned and walked away and left her.

It was a horrible thing to do but I wanted her to hate me. What I didn't know was that I was having a mental breakdown. The landlord of the pub took Madaline in for a few days and then she went and lived with her mate. I didn't go back with Jan but I still carried on seeing Madaline. I used to go to her mate Karen's place where she was stopping, spend the night shagging her and then go home all alone and sit and cry my eyes out. I was in a right state. I couldn't at the time work out what was happening to me.

It got that bad that one time I went down to Hounslow West tube station and was going to throw myself under a train. I was really going to do it. There was nothing left for me. I'd fucked so many people's lives up and mine didn't mean anything. I had no-one to turn to and I didn't know how to handle anything. I was a fucking mess. My head was also in a spin with Jan. I'd been around to see her a few times when she'd rowed with her new fella. I'd put my arms around her and comforted her and told her "that there was plenty more fish in the sea." "I don't want anyone else," she would say, "I just want you." "Jan it's too late," I said. It would never have worked but if I could have waved a magic wand and turned back time and gone back to square one I would have, believe me. There's the old saying "there's no fool like an old fool," and sadly that's very true.

People asked me if it was a big ego thing to have a 19 year old girl on my arm and to be honest, yes. I was pleased to take out a girl half my age. Wouldn't any man? But I did love her.

This particular day when I was going to commit suicide I stood on the edge of the platform in a daze and a black geezer walked past me, looked and said "man, it aint worth it." Those were his exact words and that woke me out of my nightmare. I could see no way out until this geezer had spoken to me. I somehow pulled myself together and walked out of that station and went home and cried and cried and cried. I was all alone and then it dawned on me that that was a lot of the problem. I'd always had loads of people around me. At home I had the kids and their mates in and out of the place. There was Jan and all her friends; there was all my mates from the gym and scuba diving. There was all the boxers. It was a madhouse but that was what I really missed. I missed the crowds, the noise, and the people coming in and out. I'd wrapped myself around one person and that for me was so wrong and my undoing. I didn't need a one to one and a peaceful life. I needed the crowds, the noise, and the busy-ness.

In a quiet moment I sat and wrote my first poem and I called it 'Life' and it was like lifting a ton weight off of my shoulders. On and off I'd see Madeline now and again but the intervals between our meets grew, a couple of times we planned dates and she didn't show so it was now her turn to mess me about. Then she met a fella named Tony and the next thing I heard they'd got married and now have two children. He's a local boy from Brentford who's a nice fella and funny thing; I used to know his mum. Funny how life is. When he was a nipper I used to bounce him on my knee. I remember the day because it was when Cassius Clay fought Floyd Patterson for the World Title. Whoever would have thought that one day he would meet and marry the girl I loved so much? It's uncanny.

After we split I bumped into her a couple of times shopping in Tescos. She then had a part time job in a betting shop, and I'd pop in and pass the time of day and chat about different things, nothing to serious. But then she insulted me and accused me of stalking her. She said I was freaking her out by keep coming in to see her. Then it dawned on me what a right fucking mug I'd been. I'd left a good woman and upset my kids. I'd put Madeline before everyone and for her to say that made me realize what a silly, silly, stupid prat of a bastard I'd been.

I put her above everyone and to me she was special but all she turned out to be was a special bitch. If I could put things right I really would have but unfortunately I couldn't. I'd stood up for Madeline through thick and thin. I even had a row with her stepfather after we'd split up. I just happened to ask how she was and he insulted me. I was on the warpath that day. I'd just been over to see Jan's boyfriend, who'd been bad mouthing me and had been telling people that when he saw me he was going to sort me out. I'd been to his stall over in Hounslow and he wasn't there but I did see Madeline's step dad so I pulled over and dropped the car window. I explained to him that I didn't deserve the shit he was spreading about me as I'd always treated Madeline all right. Then out of the blue he called me a cunt. I got out and told him not to be so stupid, but he wouldn't shut up and was getting louder so with that, 'Bang' I've hit him with a left hook and down he's gone. He got up and carried on cunting me off so I've hit him left, right, and he's out cold. I've looked around as he's on the floor spark out, and I noticed one of the guards was looking across the road from the barracks so I went over and asked if he'd seen what had happened. He agreed that I'd only hit him in self defence and that I hadn't stuck the boot in. All I was doing was covering my own arse in case this prick called the Old Bill and had me nicked for whacking him. He was the type to add bits on like I'd stuck the boot it.

I phoned Johnny Bloomfield and asked him to come around and make sure her step dad Pat got home all right. He agreed and I shot off. This cunt had taken my politeness as a weakness. He'd underestimated me. I'd put up with his shit for far too long. I try to love everyone and go out of my way not to upset anyone.

Hours later I got a call from Madeline calling me a bastard for what I'd done and that I was to come to 'The Beavers,' that's if I was brave enough, she growled. I walked in there and Micky Lovett, one of the local hounds, offered to watch my back. She was standing at the bar with half a dozen young geezers and as I approached her she picked up a glass ashtray from the bar and made a feeble half hearted attempt to crack me with it. She had no intention of hitting me with it; it was all a show for the watching audience. I stood firm, brushed it aside with my left hand, slapped her around the face all in one movement, and then kissed her on the lips.

Afterwards Micky Lovett described it as like a scene from the old film 'Gone With, The Wind'. I then told her "you fucked my life up. I've fucked your life up so let's call it a draw." But I know that she really loved me.

My ex wife has now been with her partner, for 16 years and we get on all right. I did hear that Madaline's mum and her step dad had split so God does pay back.

16

"KEEP YA GUARD UP"

I'm just coming up to 65 now so me becoming an old age pensioner is fast approaching. If I'm not in Audley's corner working, then me and my good mates Aiden and Roger and Jerry and Dave Evans, Pete and Kevin go to all the boxing shows. One of the last boxing shows that I promoted was at he 'Heathrow Park Hotel' it was a terrific night with Mike Read doing the cabaret. I've known Mike for years long before he was on EastEnders, he done quite a few spots for me on various shows. On the night I had the top table laid out for quite a few of the cast but most of them were late so for a while it looked a bit dodgey and I could have ended up with egg on my face. Then all of a sudden they all came in and in the end it turned out to be a good night with us all dancing together and mixing together on the dance floor. Tamzin and Lucy speed even wrote me a lovely message of thanks. When Lucy was in EastEnders me and her used to go running in our lunch break. Everyone thought we were mad in the summer we'd have sweat pouring off of us. She played "RICKKKKYS " bird in the soap, as Mike Read would call him. Peter Dean, (Pete Beale) in the soap was another boxing fan and me and him got on well. His brother Dixie Dean was a famous boxer.

I'm right into the film game now so that takes up a lot of my time. East Enders is a very big part of my life now. My eldest grandson Shane is boxing and boxes like a little pro. He's had two fights and 'as been very unlucky to lose both. One, I think he won but it was close and the other one I'd have to say the other kid just nicked it. He's like me. He suffers from terrible nerves before he gets in the ring. He's 17 now and he's a lovely kid and he helps his Uncle John out down at his gym.

John's boy Reece has just started out and, he had a very close fight with a boy from 'Chichester Boxing Club' who just got the verdict, over him. He's shaping up very well and he's just won his second fight in two rounds. You never know he could go all the way.

I'm proud of all my kids and my John has done really well. He gets more like me as he gets older. He recently organized his 40th birthday party and he is so like me. He loves organizing things. All through his life he's had so much to live up to being Harry Holland's son. I'm an extrovert and John is the opposite and very quiet and at times he can be very dour faced. As I said, as a kid he was one miserable sour faced little git. Since that time he's come out of his shell. I've always been a firm believer that boxing is real character building. It really has been the difference in him growing up and maturing. He used to be so shy, especially with the girls. He now has a couple that train down his gym and he bollocks them when they step out of line. I think he now even looks like me. He has a lot of my ways but then again he has a lot of his mum's ways which aint a bad thing. He's all for 'is mum and rightly so.

When his mum and me went through that rough patch he hated Madeline and there was a couple of times if he had of seen her God knows what he would have done to her. I was piggy in the middle but there's no way John would ever lay a hand on me and I would never touch him. We have total respect for one another. I can honestly say I couldn't have a better son. He's a man's man who's respected by all the local villains and hard men. He's respectful to women and I'm full of admiration for him.

He runs a successful gym which I don't interfere with. He runs it his way. The one thing I did do was to ask Audley Harrison to open it on the first day. Unfortunately I was away filming with East Enders so I couldn't be there but that didn't stop Audley from turning up and making it a day to remember but then again, that's the mark of the man. He turned up on his own and the kids loved him and all the adults wanted to buy him a drink. He was loved by everyone.

John has another son, Kane whose just coming up to his 14th birthday.

My Mandy, my eldest, as I said before, is so straight. She's a great mum to her two boys, Jordon and Corby who are both football mad like their dad, Ricky. Who trains the Staines under elevens.

Tracey the youngest is a diamond and also has two lovely children, Shane who boxes and Lacey, her daughter who's coming on 15, and no doubt with her charm and good looks will break a few hearts. I must drive my Tracey mad with the amount of things I asked her to do. But that's what daughters are for when you get older. The rules are that you spoil them when they've young and they look after you when you're old. It's simple?

So, I class myself a very lucky man to have such a lovely bunch of grandchildren. I see them all some time or other, at least once a week.

There's been one or two women that's been in and out of my life recently but nothing regular. I think I'm still looking for one that will understand me and put up with me. I'm not ever against getting married again if the right one came along, then who knows?

I still go to the lodge a lot and have some great friends there. My son in law, Paul, has just been initiated into the Masons and I'm proud of that.

I still see Freddie Foreman, but sadly, Joey Pyle is suffering from Motor Neurons disease which is not a very nice thing to have. I went to his 70th birthday bash a few months back and all I can say is that he's a very brave man. The party was held at his house and all the chaps came along to see him and wish him well. I had a good chat that night with Brian Emett who's been a pal of Joe's for years. Now, Brians in his 70s, and he's still fighting he won't back down from no one. Just recently a young kid got a bit loud and Brian sorted him out. He said to me " Harry I've been around to long to be intimidated by these youngsters. I ain't having it" Joe's a special man who I've always got on well with.

I've worked with Joe Junior on a few shows and he's a nice boy. The new generation of lovable rogues would have to include my good friend Dominic Negus. I was in Audley Harrison's corner when they fought at Wembley, which Audley won over 6 rounds on points. Dominic, was a very exciting fighter who didn't give a fuck for anyone, who was managed by my old mucker Frank Maloney. He had 15 contests winning 10. Outside the ring he's a top bloke and I've had some good nights with him. We went out to the States to watch Prince Naseem fight and we went to Alcatraz prison and both joked that we wouldn't have liked to have done any bird in there. Another time I met him in the 'MGM Grand Hotel' and he spotted me and grabbed me and lifted me clean up above his head. He is as strong as a lion." Harry Holland" He was shouting at the top of his voice, the Yanks were looking at him as if he was some nutcase. He's a larger then life character who's fearless and scared of no-one but as a heart of gold. I'm proud to be his friend.

I also like the theatre. I've been to some musicals that would make the hair on the back of your neck stand up on end. Shows like 'Phantom of the Opera' and 'Chicago'. I tell my mates about so and so show and they look at me as if to say "what the fuck's he on about?" But for me it's a real buzz.

I don't know what it is but I feel as if my life 'as gone on a bit of a curve. From a child I was sexually abused so I went out and done the manly things like box, then bounced and scuba dived. So it was all about me proving my masculinity. Then there's all the women. I've gone full circle now. I really enjoy the theatre and the next stop is to go to the opera or to a ballet. I'm serious; maybe that is the bit of Delboy coming out in me.

I still see some of my old boxers. I often see Rocky Kelly and Andy Till and James Cook who has just got married after 24 years of courting his lovely lady. He's also just appeared in a T.V. documentary about his job working with kids in Hackney, East London. He came across so well in that programme that I've nothing but praise for James. I'll make a bold forecast but I reckon he is destined for bigger and better things after appearing in that show. Maybe an M.B.E. on the way? The one I'd like to meet up with again is Trevor Smith. We lost touch a few years back but I'd love to have a beer and a chat with him again.

I see Charlie Magri at shows, along with Alan Minter. His son, Ross, is doing well in the pro ranks so look out for him. He's one for the future.

When I look back and think about all the boxers I've worked with and watched at close quarters I'd have to say that Billy Walker would have to be one of my all time favourites. Billy and his wife Jackie lived out in Tenerife for a while and when we bumped into one another we'd stop and chat. Now that man could sell out venues like no-one else. The fans loved him. He dipped out of the limelight years ago but is now on the Boxing Board of Control.

His brother, George was the money man and done well out of the pub game but just above him I would have to put Mohammed Ali. He was out of this world. He was so fast, strong, and technically he had everything. Look at some of his old fights and you'll see a master at work. I remember when he fought Cleveland Williams just before he went off into the American army and he threw text book shots all through that fight. That was Ali at his best. He then had a 3 year lay off, had one warm up fight and then fought Smokin' Joe Frazier. I think the lay off beat Ali that night, not Joe Frazier, but I'll take nothing away from Smokin' Joe. He was one of the greats as well. Ali then came back later and beat Frazier in the "Thrilla in Manila."

He also bashed up big George Foreman out in Zaire in the "dope on a rope" fight. Ali allowed Big George to come onto him in those early rounds until George had punched himself out while Ali leant back on the ropes and took all that George could throw on his high held gloves. A con man at his best but that was Ali. He was his own man. He then came alive in that fight and trapped a near exhausted George and the rest is history as George was knocked out.

I remember watching one of the Ali v Frazier fights at the Odeon and Chris Finnegan's missus was there in a pair of tight fitting hot pants and she did have a beautiful pair of legs. Nearly all the audience were more interested in looking at her and trying to catch a peak up her shorts than the action in the ring being beamed back from the States! I remember having a conversation with Chris about Les Southey and he looked at me and said " I'd rather fight Bob Foster again for the world title then fight Les.

I still see Chris at shows. Kevin his brother, to me was the better boxer plus he's a nutcase with a fantastic personality. Kevin is now an artist and at times dresses up in the striped jumper with an earring and a beret and speaks in this French accent. He only needs the onions and he'd be complete. At a show a geezer started getting a bit load with Kevin so I stepped in to calm things down. I think this bloke saw Kevin as a bit of an easy touch. I took the fella to one side and explained to him who he was rowing with. I told him that Kevin had fought Marvin Hagler twice in close fights. But I don't think it registered. Kevin then came over and in broken English said " Harry what eeezz za matter did the man vont zee fisty cuffs?)

"Kevin, why I you talking like that? I know you're not French" and he laughed. Up until recently I used to bump into Terry Downes. Now that is one funny character and he has me in stitches. It was his 70th birthday recently and he's now the 'President of the Home Counties Ex-Boxers' Association'. There was a letter in the 'Boxing News' only the other week stating that Terry must be the oldest ex world champion still alive. We were good pals for years and some of his exploits are legendary. He was so rude to some people but he just didn't care. We were at a show once and this geezer kept looking over at Terry and the group he was with.

"Excuse me mate is that Terry Downes over there?" asked the Scouse fella.

"Yes it is mate," I replied.

"Any chance of introducing me to him as I saw you talking to him earlier and he's an all time hero of mine?"

"He'll insult ya mate, he's in one of them moods," I told him.

The kid wouldn't listen so I took him over to meet Terry.

"Terry, this is Brian."

"Hello Terry pleased to meet you."

"Fucking Scouser, there's nothing good to come out of Liverpool. Even the football teams are shit" And that was it. He tore this fella to pieces. The bloke loved it and thought Terry was joking but that was Terry. He didn't give a fuck who he upset.

I saw him at Dave Boy Green's book launch and I accidentally walked past Terry not noticing he was there. Then he growled, "that's it, don't talk to me ya miserable git, blow me out." He never stops moaning, but I love him to bits. Dave Boy Green's doing well with his book and he looks well.

I try to keep myself busy these days and I always find something to do. I still feel the urge to come back and do some promoting and I may still do one day. Who knows?

The last boxer I had was Courtney Fry. He was 'Commonwealth Gold Medallist.' He'd won 3 A.B.A. Titles and he was more than good. He won 8 out of 8 with me as a pro. The next fight he had he lost to Oval McKenzie, which is no disgrace, as he'd beaten Oval before. I put him with Chris Saniger but its not working out for the pair of them which is a shame because it's a choker because Courtney 'as so much potential and Chris is such a nice bloke. I don't know what's gone on there? Courtney is a lovely kid but don't right him off because he could still go all the way.

I now also put on cabaret shows a couple of times at year at 'The Winning Post' venue in Twickenham. You get a 3 course dinner and a couple of look-alike acts. It's great fun and it keeps everyone together. Lots of my friends come along. There's ex boxers, villains, actors, it a great night. I've had Diana Ross, Roy Orbison, Rod Stewart, Elvis, and others. The people who come love it.

It keeps me away from boxing. Don't get me wrong I love the sport but the state it's in at the moment aint the same sport I fell in love with. It's all changed. With no T.V. deals it's hard to make a living. The boys at the top have it sewn up and good luck to them. Someone starting off today as a promoter would find it a real struggle. The safety aspect in boxing in some people's views is way over the top. Personally, take amateur boxing, when they introduced head guards, well, for me that finished the sport. A lot of the thrills and the action and the punches landing is taken away by the use of head protectors. The thing with brain damage is with the rotation of the brain but head guards don't prevent that. It's done more by the shock wave than by the power. That's how I look at head guards. They could possibly cause more problems than they prevent.

There aint many fighters who excite me these days. Ricky Hatton I hear you say, but he's just one. Amir Khan's another one. He's good but just how good? I think he's being nursed along so let's see how good he really is when he gets in with someone who can take a shot and more importantly, can throw a shot.

I had Rocky Kelly turned pro at 18 and he would have fought anyone. He didn't give a fuck. The good thing is he seemed to have near on the whole country behind him. He had the talent to go all the way, and nearly did. Chris Sanigar from Bristol is one of the up and coming promoters who's swum against the tide for so long but he works bloody hard and he's, I'm glad to say, getting there. While we're on Bristol I was asked to promote Jane Couch the woman boxer's first fight. She was the first girl to get a pro –boxers licence. I turned it down, because I had strong views on women's boxing. But I ended up doing the matchmaking for her first fight. After that we became good friends. She's a right character. Another good lady pro, is 'Cathy The Bitch Brown' she's a pretty little girl and a good boxer. She's not long won a title, so good luck to her, women's boxing as come on leaps and bounds and as come on stronger. Even I've been converted to it. I didn't use to take it seriously but I watched two girls, box the other week and technically they were good plus they went toe to toe. The way it's going I think it has a bright future. Now also you not only have lady boxers but there's now lady MCs. Lisa Budd is one such lady who's very good at her job and lovely looking with it. I took her with me to a few boxing shows and she came with me to The Ewbank- Benn, fight. At the time she was Mickey Duff's secretary and he see me and her at this show and decides that he's going to sack her as he saw me and her friendship as a conflict of interests. The thing was we never spoke about one another's business, to each other. It went to court and she won her claim for unfair dismissal and copped eight grand. Every time I used to see him after that he used to say. "Harry how's your girlfriend?" Lisa is a lovely girl and still a good mate of mine. While on MCs John McDonald had done well for himself. He first started out as a photographer when I was with Frank Warren. he took some fantastic pictures of Rocky and Creamy, and Andy Till in the ring. Then one day I was having a chat with him and he mentioned that he signed up to do 'The Knowledge' to become a London black cab driver. He also said that he was going to give it a go as an MC and go along the lines of the Americans With "LETS GET READY TO RUUUUUUMMMMMMMBBBLLLLE" and all that palaver. To a lot of peoples amazement he done it, and he's doing well so good luck to him. He also went on to do 'The Knowledge' Another London cab driver associated with boxing is old Charlie Shoreys pal and time keeper, Danny Peacock. He must be well into his eighties now but he still drives a cab. The last fight I saw him at as a timekeeper was the Bruno- McCaul fight at Wembley. Danny at one time used to look after a few of Joe Pyles fighters.

All in all if I can beat this illness and keep fit I'll be happy. One boxer I did miss out on and I'm sure would have made a big difference in which direction my life went, was Frank Bruno. I knew him from early on in his amateur career when he boxed at 'The Sir Phillip Game Club' with Freddie Rix. I chatted to him at a show once and could just see him turning pro and fulfilling his potential. But financially he was way out of my league. You knew he was going to someone with the financial backing. But it was worth a try, because as they say a faint heart never won nothing. He's such a gentleman. At one of my shows the woman taking the money on the door charged Frank, twenty pounds to get in, she didn't realize who he was and being the gent he is he didn't want to cause a scene so he paid. When I thanked him for coming, he pointed out that he'd been charged to get in. "Ye ye I'll sort ya dough out later." I said to him and I could tell it had wound him up. All night long I kept promising to pay him back and in the end we had a laugh when him and me had our photo done together with him holding this ticket up. I have a small place over in Tenerife, which I go out to quite a bit, and I have some good friends over there. Two right characters I drink with are 'Phil the Pill' and 'Stan the Man' Phil got his name not by being a drug dealer, but from when I took him out one day on an early morning run and he left me for dead I joked with him that he must have been on the gear and that he'd been out the night before and stashed some pills on the route. Their big wind up was to dress up as the Captains of big cruise ships and tell exaggerated tales of life on the high seas, the thing was people would believe them. Their best one was when they dressed up as Concorde pilots and got pissed as farts in a bar and told everyone that they were flying that night, out to Bahrain or somewhere, the look on some peoples faces they were so convincing. Stan is a very funny Scouser who loves a pound note and loves the crack. His best friend over here is the comedian Stan Boardman and even appeared on, 'This is Your Life' with him. But at the moment he's in a bit of bother and he's banged up and awaiting trial. He hasn't got a bad bone in his body so I hope he's out soon.

I'm going on a cruise over Christmas and then I'm back to see my doctor and then who knows? You might see me again climbing through the ropes. Maybe taking on Sylvester Stallone in 'Rocky 8' on the silver screen. Now there's a fairy tale from Brentford, via EastEnders, to Hollywood. I have a simple saying, "Don't hold ya breath, enjoy every moment in life." I'd like people to think about me when I'm gone and say. "He was a lad that Harry."

EPILOGUE

Sadly as I write this my dear friend Joey Pyle has sadly passed away. God bless you Joe my friend your be sadly missed by us all.

Also Michael Sprott beat Audley Harrison in a fight shown live on TV. Will he come back? Watch this space?

MUCKERS

FIGHTERS MANAGED

Barry Ellis, Heavyweight, Max Wallace, Light Middleweight, Richard Thomas, Light Middleweight, Tony Williams, Light Middleweight, Sylvester Mitte, Welterweight and also a British Challenger, Eammon McAuley, Lightweight and ex ABA Champion, Andy Strong, Cruiserweight British Champion, Des Vaughan, Heavyweight, Ally Forbes Light Middleweight, British Champion, Gary Booker, Middleweight, Darren Murphy Light Middle, Dave Boy Fallung, Welterweight, Jim Talbot, Light Welterweight, Colin McMullan, Bantamweight, Wee Barry, Light Welterweight, Ray Webb, Middleweight, Courtney Fry who was 3 times ABA Champion, Commonwealth Champion and 9 out of 10 times with me as a pro, Martin Smith, Light Middleweight, Steve McArthy, Light Heavyweight, Leigh Wicks, Welterweight, Adrian Riley, Welter, Mark Dinidge, Light Welter, Steve McGovern, Light Welter, Winston Spencer, Welter, Mark Hilden, Welter, Nicky Bardel, Light Welter, Vernon Vanrail, Lightweight, James Cook, British Super Middleweight Champion and European Champion, Gary Hobbs, Middleweight Southern Area Champion, Rocky Kelly, Welterweight Southern Area Champion and British Title Challenger, Nicky Harrison, Light Middleweight, Tommy Eastwood, Heavyweight, Neville Smith, Light Heavyweight, Cliff Eastwood, Light Welterweight, Tony Rabetts, Light Middleweight, Dennis O'Brien, Light Middleweight, Dean Savory, Welterweight, Andy Till, British Light Middleweight Champion and WBC Continental Champion and European Challenger, Trevor Smith, Southern Area

141

Welterweight Champion and British Title Challenger, Serge Fane, Light Heavyweight Southern Area Champion and British Title Challenger, Steve McCarthy, Southern Area Light Heavyweight Champion and also Light Heavyweight Champion of Britain, Simon Harris, Southern Area Champion, Tony Burke, Middle Southern Area Champion, Derek Myers, Light Heavyweight, Funso Banjo Heavyweight, Simon Eubanks Welterweight, W.O. Wilson, Light Middle Southern Area Champion and British Light final eliminator,?????Vic Wright, Light welter, Carlos Chase, Light Heavy, Adrian Chase, Welterweight.

The above were all the fighters that I actually managed during the course of my career.

Now I will give you the amateur boxers that I trained during my course as a boxing trainer at amateur.

Brian Hide, Peter Smith, George Rabbetts, John Holland, Roy Rabbetts, Tony Rabbetts, Paul Keating, Billy Austin, Roy Hilton, Paul Hilton, Grantley Beccles, Gary Hobbs, Jimmy Prenderghast, Snowey Kim Harper, Mark Cammack, Jaz Ark, Richard Trump, Dennis O'Brien, Rocky Kelly, Micky Harrison, Mark Williams, Spencer Williams, Tony Williams, Dean Savory, Ray Savory, Lee Fitzwalter, Stuart Cooper, Paul Klyne, Wayne Welter, Stevie Welter, Tony Wells, John Wells, George Walker, Earl Edwards, Richard Edwards, Clive Banaf, Dave Yeardley, Max Wallace, Eammon McCauley, Dave Pilgrim, Chrissie Dean, Billie Dixon, Russell Donovan, Grant Donovan, Lee Dewbury, Gary Dakin, Jason Fox, Paul Friday, Colin Cawley, Stevie Franklin, Mark Clarke, Ronnie Shillingford, Gerry Shillingford, Peter Lipscombe, Lloyd Mahoney, Martin Herdman, Brian Griffiths, Mark Pollington, Steve Pollington, Ian Middleton, Chris O'Rielly, Barry O'Rielly, Vince McCarthy, Wayne Buckley, John Bryant, Cliff Cowan, Ralph Young, Jason Bartlett, Stuart Hope, Michael Harris, Mark Worsefold, Paul Christmas, Mark Mariner, Jason Mariner, John Humphries, Brian Tough, Lee Williams, Mark Whistler, Charlie Fitzgerald, Vincent Burke, John Downing, Ray White, Trevor Boyle, Billy Griggs, Steve Yowarth,

Robin Cox, Steve Taylor, Tony Evans, Garry Aitken, Colin Tindall, Mark Gator, Devon Bailey, Bob Flynn, Carl Harrison. Those were the amateur boxers.

Boxers that I worked with that I never managed.

Audley Harrison, I'm his cut man now, Colin Cracknell, John Conti, John Stracey, Charlie Magri, Barry Jones (ex WBO world superfeather weight champion), Lloyd Honeyghan, Dennis Andreas, Alan Minter, Nicky Cook, Ross Minter, Dave Boy Green, Frank Bruno, Lennox Lewis, Derek Williams, James Oyebola, Robert Lloyd Taylor, Ricky Hatton, Wally Swift Junior, Joe Bugner, Joe Bugner Junior, Andrew Lowe, Mat Skelton, Robert W. Smith, John Lewis, Glen McCory, Nigel Benn, Terry Marsh, Tommy Farr, Danny McAlindon, Lester Jacobs, Colin Jones, Kirkland Laing, Wally Angus and many more to remember. These are all boxers that I have worked with at some time or other during my boxing career.

Friends who I would personally like to mention

Peter and Pam Dakin, Trevor and Barbara Davies, John Rowlands, Bat and Josie, Fred Pearman and Jill, Les Hogg and Maureen, Jeffrey Johnston and Marge, Bub Plummer and Chris, Carol and Mark, Angie Payne and Glen, Carol and Barry, Jim and Bev, Terry and Sheila, Curly and Ruth, Eddie, Reeves and Sue, Kay and Richard, Bob Flynn and Ellie, Maria and Roger, Janet and Gerald, Larry and Cheryl, Coreene, Sam and Mark, Ron Griffiths, Bella, Mark Cammack and Caroline, Dave Yeardley and Jan, Dave Yeardley Junior and Gloria, Christine and Clive, Bill Fox and Jane, Sid and Mitzi, Graham Betts and Bev, Peter Norrington and Jan, Tracey Davies and Carlton, Lindsey Davies, Lisa, Chris Davies, Carmen, Joan and Roy Rowe, Dave Wells and Hazel, Dave Moles and Val, Dave Stairs and Val, Tony O'Brien and June, Bobby Hutchens and Jackie, Ron Ede and Flo, Lisa Ede and Stuart, Chris Ede and Tony Jenkins, Julia Ede, Gordon Ede, Mike Williamson and Jean, Sarah, Michaela, Acker and Pats, Rufus and Jan, Les and Jackie, Mark Trump and Amber and all the beautiful girls at Bunters Cafe, Maurice and Helen, Harry Rolfe and Hillary, Joey Barwick and Maura, Gerald

Barwick and Angie, Fred Savory and Shirley, Ted, Samson and Maureen, Selina and Bill, John Blower and Sandra, Sally Bloomfield, Kelly, Dave, Natalie, Stevie Allan, Dave Mudge, Dave Taylor, Alfie Belchambers, Harry Belchambers, Laurie and Bob, Alby George, Arthur Richardson, John Moles, Angie Worsfold, Mike and Jean from the Six Bells, Robert Chick, Ross Hemsworth, Paul Crockford who was also the manager of Level 42, a lovely man, Dave Evans and Viv, Aiden Holloway and Sue, Roger Collins and Simon, Pete Kinsilla and Paul, Rob, Jamie and Kelly, Kevin Kinziller, Timmy Caron, Gary Clarke, Tony Montana, Richard Atkins, George Savea, Roger Moody, Ron Fairbrother, Stan the Man, Phil, the Pill, Gary and John, Richard and Gaynor, Richard and Anita, Colin and Wendy, Mike the President, Steve, Allan, Dennis New, Joe at Bobby's Bar and all my mates at Springers Bar, my Masonic friends, such as Cliff Shaw, Kevin Tidy, Frank O'Neill, Roger Conway, Ken, Steve Betts, Tony Miles, David Conns, Alan Spear, Mark Cammack, Glen Cammack, Alan Swaby, Roger Collins, Martin Ashby, Adrian, Philip Harrison, Chris Cordes, Wayne Buckley, Charlie Loveridge and the boys, and if I've missed out anyone I apologise.

Managers and Promotors that I've dealt with

Alex Steene, Greg Steene, Frank Warren, Micky Duff, Terry Lawless, Frank Maloney, Barney Eastwood, Barry Hearn, Tommy Gilmore, Dennis Hobson, Jim Evans, Dave Currivan George Carmen, Jack Bishop, Pat Brogan, Tony Burns, Dave Coldwell, Jane Couch, Pat Cordell, Wally Dixon, Jack Dougherty, Joe Frater, Dave Garside, Jess Harding, Chris Sanigar, Jamie Sanigar, Hazel Bruno, Jenny Griffin, Johnny Ingle, Brendon Ingle, John Merton, Alec Morrison, Joey Pyle, John Felds, Bruce Baker, Keith Walker, Mike Shinfield, Steve Wood, Alan Mortlake, Waddy Swift Senior, Eugene Maloney, Pat Healey, John Gaynor, Jack Tricket, Tommy Miller, rest in peace.

The trainers that I've been involved with in the boxing.

My friend, Johnny Bloomfield, Harry Monger, Peter Snowshell, Fred Savory, John Scott, Brian Lawrence, Brian Dawson, Brian Wells, Paul

Mum and me with James
Cook's Lonsdale Belt

Me, Bill Moss and Colin
Cracknell

John Conteh and John Banham who was 5-times police boxing champion and is sadly no longer with us

Creamy with John Bloomfield after he'd been sparing with Joe Bugner

Alex Steene, Tommy Farr, me and Greg Steene at our Porchester Hall promotion

Nigel v Robbie Simms which I promoted

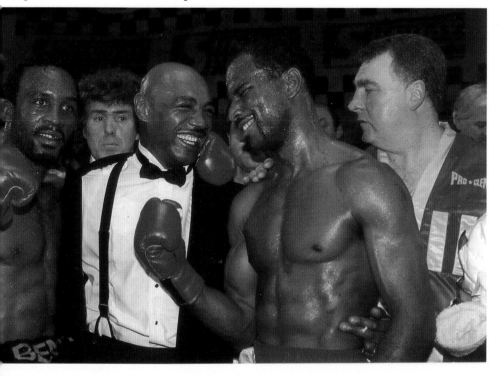

Sugar Ray Leonard one of the all time greats

Joe Pyle Junior, Joey Pyle, Roberto Durran and me at 'Wallys' bar in Twickenham

With champion James Cook down at the gym

Tony Burke, Andy Till and W.O. Wilson 3 Southern Area champions

Amir Khan and my grandson Shane

Cathy the Bitch Brown, the first girl pro boxer I managed

Down at my Johns 'Westside Gym'

Courtney Fry and Audley Harrison

Audley and his trainer Thell Torrance

Barbra Windsor with all us stallholders

Michael Greco and Daniella Westbrooke

Martin Kemp

Steve (Phil)

Tazmin

With Shane Richie outside the 'Vic'

'Footballer's Wives' with Gary Iucy and Brian Nichols

On my stall

Fiona Wright, who worked with me at 'Winners Worlwide' and wrote a lovely message on the back of her photo, it read; 'Harry, I'll never forget the night we spent together. Lots of love Fiona Wright'. Was I her 12 times a night man? I wished.

The grandchildren at a wedding

Shane, Reece. Lacey, Kane, Jordan and Colby. I'm so proud of them all

The gang from
Tenerife with 'Stan
the Man' and 'Phil the
Pill'

Me and Dominic
Negas with 'Alcatraz
Prison' in the back-
ground

'Strictly Come Dancing' with Dave Courtney

With the Queen Mum, hidden is my Lidls carrier bag

The yearly re-union of 'The Fools and Horses' fans day. You get look-alikes and some of the stars of the show turn up.

Me in the Lodge. On the right is my son-in-law Paul, to the left is Toby his friend

Cook, John Emmes, Tony Simms, Alan Booth, Jacky Bowers, Paul Boyce, David Bradley, John Breen, Michael Brennan, Nigel Christian, Ronnie Davies, Tanya Fawcett, Philip Fondu, Steve James, Dai Gardner, Jimmy Gill, Mike Hill, Pat Lynch, Robert McCracken, Jim McDonald, Paul Newman, Nobby Nobbs, Terry O'Neil, Steve Poddard, Howard Rainey, Mark Roe, Kevin Saunders, Glenroy Taylor, Tex Woodwood, John Ashton, Neil Bowers, Roy Hilder, Dean Powell, Wayne Barker, Les Southey, Micky Kinsell.

My friends that I've dealt with in the United States

The late Chris Dundee, Angelo Dundee, Tell Torrence, Kenny, Trevor Birbeck, rest in peace, Dan Duva ,and Donald Trump.

A special thank you to British Boxing Board of Control

Mr Simon Block, Mr Robert Smith, Di Corp, Bob Lonkhurst, and all the Board officials.

Referees

Larry O'Connell, Dave Parris, Micky Vann, Paul Thomas, Ken Curtis, John Lewis, Roland Dakin and many more.

My TV Commentators and MCs.

My friend Steve Holdsworth and John McDonald.

The TV producers that I owe a lot to

Roger Moody, John Moody, Brian Barwick, Gary Norman, Ian Dark,

Sports Writers that I have dealt with during the course of my involvement in boxing.

Colin Hart, Steve Bunts, Ron Lewis, Lawrence Lustig, Ronny Shillingford, Steve Lillas, Simon Smith, Chris Kempson, Claude Abrams and George Zeleny.

Men Of Respect

Alex Steene, rest in peace, Charlie Kray, rest in peace, Tony Lambrianou rest in peace, and now unfortunately, Joe Pyle. Freddie Foreman, Charlie Richardson, Eddie Richardson, Brian Emmit, Dave Courtney, Roy Shaw, Jimmy, John Nash, Franky Frazer, Dave Appleby, Roy Dennis, Lenny McLean, rest in peace, Dominic Negus, Dennis New, John Binden, rest in peace, and any that I've forgotten I apologise to.

My Friends in The Bill

Chris Ellison, Mark Winnett, Tony, Gary Lucy, and Graham Cole.

My friends in films

Ray Winstone, Bob Mackay, Christina Richie, Joan Collins, etc.

All the royalty I've met.

The Queen, the Royal Premier, I've met her down EastEnders as well, the Queen Mother at St. James Palace, Princess Margaret I met at Kensington Palace, Lord Lindley, Barbara Cartland, Duke of Kent, etc.

Actors

Shaun Williamson, Shane Richie, John, Ricky Groves, Cliff, plays Minty, Joel plays Jack, Nadia Swahali, Mark Banahan, Michael Greco, Dean Gaffney, Cliff Metcalfe, Troy Titmuss, Martine McCutcheon, Patsy Palmer, Daniella Westlake, Tamsin Outhwaite, Carla who plays Dawn, Barbara Windsor, June Brown, Wendy Richards, Martin Kemp. The stall holders my friends, Madaline, Ina, Lila, Maggi, John, Doreen, Lou, Nicky, Sara, Jayne, Ruth, Karen, Martha, Darryl, Paul, Orich, Carl, Lloyd and Luke.

My special SA friends

Pommie, Astrid, Penny, Jo, Frank, Pat, Bill, Gareth, Glenn, Mike, Phil, Dave, John Carney, Pete, Ray, Paul and many more and apologies to anyone I've left out.

All my friends at snooker

I met Jimmy White, Tony Meo, John Virgo, and Henry West who first introduced me to them all. He was the first man in the business.

146

Wrestling

The Parks Brothers.

To all the girls I have loved and may not have loved before

Madaline, Gay, April, Tracey, Coreene, Kathy, Cathy D, Kathy, Chris, Judy, June, Becky, Susie B, Maria W, Ann, Mitzy, Rose, Liza D, Liz, Christine, Marg, Doreen, Kim, Nadia S, Sue B, Joanne, Sammy, Angie, Debby Q, Sharon B, Sharon, Sara J, Julie B, Gaynor M, Sandy Lock, Jenny E.

Pop Stars

Chuck Berry, Shakin Stevens, Crazy Cavern, The Impalas, Gene Vincent, Bill Hayley, Screaming Lord Sutch, Little Richard, Dave Meadows, Lee Tracey, Matchbox, Wild Angels, Joe Brown, Level 42, Marty Wild, Roger Daltry.

Respected Stuntmen that I have worked with.

Tom Lucey, Nosher Powell, Gary Powell, Steve Wittings, Greg Powell, Derek Lee, Brian Nicholls and Denise Ryan.

Last, but by no means least obviously, my family.

Mandy and Ricky, John and Darcey, Tracey and Paul, Jeff and Marg, Dave and Steven, Kay and Peter. And the grandchildren, which is Shane, Jordon and Colby, Reece and Kane and Lacey. My sister Kay with greatest respect, my half sister, Josey, and Tony, Jan and Paul. My Aunts, Eileen and Les, Shirley Rogers, Brian Rogers, Les and Shirl, Becky and Phil, Danny, Beverley, and Rebecca.

Love to you all xxx

SCRAPBOOK

LONDON AMATEUR BOXING ASSOCIATION

(PATRON: THE RT. HON. THE LORD MAYOR OF LONDON)

PRESIDENT: W. H. ROBINSON
HON. SECRETARY: M. O'BRIEN
(to whom all correspondence should be addressed)
LIFE VICE-PRESIDENTS: H. A. HADDEN, J. H. LEWIS, N. R. COEL, C. J. HAWKES, K. E. L. SHORT

68 CENTRAL BUILDINGS,
24 SOUTHWARK STREET,
LONDON, SE1 1TY.
01-407 2194/5

MO'B/GG/JR

17th December, 1982

H. Holland Esq.,
356, Convent Way,
Southall,
Middlesex.

Dear Mr. Holland,

REGISTRATION WITHDRAWN

Information has been received that you have participated in Professional Boxing, contrary to the Rules & Regulations of the Association.

At the L.A.B.A. Council Meeting on Tuesday, 14th December 1982, it was decided that your Registration as an A.B.A. Coach be withdrawn forthwith. Therefore, you are not permitted to take any further part in Amateur Boxing.

Also, you are requested to return your Registration Book to this office immediately. A stamped addressed envelope is enclosed for this purpose.

Yours sincerely,

(HON. SECRETARY)

enclos:

copy to Hogarth A.B.C.

MIRAGE
WINDSOR

IN ASSOCIATION WITH

WINNERS WORLDWIDE BOXING LTD
& HARRY HOLLAND BOXING PROMOTIONS

PRESENT

ON MONDAY 22ND APRIL

OUR LAST BOXING SHOW OF THE SEASON

BOXING • DINNER • CABARET

featuring

W.O. WILSON vs. IAN CHANTLER
plus FULL SUPPORTING BOUTS

DOUBLE CABARET - Featuring

HARRY SCOTT - *Comedian*
Plus DISCO

TICKETS: £40 EACH (INCLUDING 3 COURSE SET DINNER)
DOORS OPEN 7.30 PM

Tickets available from:

MIRAGE, WILLIAM STREET, WINDSOR	– 0753 856222
WINNERS WORLDWIDE	– 071-354 3414
HARRY HOLLAND	– 081-890 4030
CHAS CORKERY	– 071-286 8183
ROGER COLLINS	– 081-579 4389
CECIL BEAST	– 081-689 5452

Harry Holland & Winners Worldwide

PRESENT

The Battle of Battersea II

Championship Professional Boxing

WELTERWEIGHT ELIMINATOR & SOUTHERN AREA CHAMPIONSHIP 10×3 min rounds **TREVOR** POWER HOUSE **SMITH** CHAMPION (HARLOW) V **MICKEY** THE HIT MAN **HUGHES** CHALLENGER (CAMDEN TOWN)	SUPER MIDDLEWEIGHT ELIMINATOR 10×3 min rounds **JAMES COOK** (PECKHAM) *THE ONLY MAN TO DEFEAT MICHAEL WATSON* V **SLUGGER O'TOOLE** (SHEFFIELD) *FROM THE HEROL GRAHAM STABLE*
SOUTHERN AREA LT HEAVYWEIGHT CHAMPIONSHIP 10×3 min rounds **SERGE FAME** (PADDINGTON) V **GLAZZ CAMPBELL** (BROCKLEY)	*THE MOST EXCITING BOXER IN BRITAIN* WELTERWEIGHT CONTEST — 8×3 min rounds THE EXPLOSIVE **ROCKY KELLY** (FULHAM) V **WINSTON WRAY** (BOLTON)

PLUS 3 CONTESTS FEATURING

EAMONN McAULEY (Ex ABA CHAMPION) *THE MOST EXCITING IRISH FIGHTER SINCE BARRY McGUIGAN*	**MAX WALLACE** (BARNES) *MR ENTERTAINMENT*	**CARLOS CHASE** (BUSHEY) *DESTINED FOR TOP HONOURS*

THURSDAY 28th SEPT   Doors open: 7.30pm   Boxing : 8.00pm
At THE LATCHMERE LEISURE CENTRE, BATTERSEA, SW11

TICKETS: RINGSIDE £50 · OUTER RINGSIDE £40 · BLEACHER £30 · BACK OF HALL £20

AVAILABLE FROM

HARRY HOLLAND 01-890 4030 WINNERS WORLDWIDE 01-354 3414 JOHN BLOOMFIELD 01-890 4030	BRIAN HILL 01-769 2218 TREVOR SMITH 0279 659321 ROCKY KELLY 01-385 6276	BRENDAN INGLE 0742 423392 LES SOUTHEY 0895 54719 DAVE DAVIS 01-455 8188

BOOK EARLY FOR THIS EXCITING SHOW—IT'S VALUE FOR MONEY

WINNERS WORLDWIDE LTD & HARRY HOLLAND
BOXING PROMOTIONS

TREVOR "POWER HOUSE" SMITH.

Trevor "Power House" Smith from Harlow, the current Southern
Area Welterweight Champion meets Peterborough's very
experienced Lennie Gloster over 8 rounds. Smith aged 26 and
unbeaten in 13 professional contests won the Southern Area
crown in his last outing on January 24th at the Latchmere
Leisure Centre. He stopped brave Ian John-Lewis in the eighth
round of a wildly exciting see-saw battle to win the vacant
crown. This contest has rightly been described as one of the
greatest small hall contests of all time. Trevor turned
professional in 1985 and opened with a six round points
victory over Londoner, Simon Paul at the Heathrow Park Hotel,
Longford. Notable scalps include: Paul Wetter, Claude Rossi,
Courtney Phillips, though Welshman Kevin Mortimer, Shamus
Casey and Rory Callagham. Facing Trevor this evening is
Peterborough's Lennie Gloster in what will be his 50th
professional outing. Born in the West Indies in 1956, Gloster
turned professional here in 1983, he is a former holder of the
Southern Area Light Welterweight title. Although he has faced
among others:- Dave Dent, Yony McKinzie, Tony Adams, Gary
Stretch, Chris Blake, Errol McDonald, George Collins, Peter
Crook and Pat "BlackFlash" Barratt (new British Light
Welterweight Champion). His fight against Micky Hughes on the
28th September at the "Battle of Battersea II" should be full
of fireworks. Hughes has only lost two out of 18 fights:
providing he wins this fight, Trevor will be lined up for a
crack at the British Title.

Halesmere House • 59 Islington Park Street • London N1 1QB
Tel: 01-354 3414 • Fax: 01-704 0213
•
71 Beech Road • Bedfont • Middlesex
Tel: 01-890 4030

WINNERS WORLDWIDE LTD & HARRY HOLLAND
BOXING PROMOTIONS
·
Reply to: London ☐   Middlesex ☐

Aged 29, James Cook will be fighting at the "Battle of
Battersea II" under a new category - Super Middleweight.

A true professional, he has no time for some of the "frills"
and nicknames often associated with fighters of his standing.
He enjoys a good working relationship with manager and trainer
Harry Holland. Having turned pro in 1982, he has had 13 wins
in 23 fights and is the only person to have beaten Michael
Watson at Wembley in 1986. Since he joined the Holland
stable, his career has demonstrated a very promising and
positive direction; this was clearly shown in his last fight
in March 1989, against "Golden Boy" Errol Christie who was
knocked down twice before Cook took the decision in the 5th.

His ability to fight in both middleweight and
supermiddleweight categories means Cook is only 3 fights away
from the World Middleweight Title.

WINNERS WORLDWIDE LTD & HARRY HOLLAND
BOXING PROMOTIONS
·
Reply to: London ☐   Middlesex ☐

NEWSFLASH.

Harry Holland and Winners Worlwide Boxing Promotions have now
signed former British Cruiserweight Champion Andy Straughan.
The Winners/Holland stable are lining him up for a shot at the
World Title against Glen McCory in the near future.

**WINNERS WORLDWIDE LTD & HARRY HOLLAND
BOXING PROMOTIONS**

•

Reply to: London ☐   Middlesex ☐

HARRY HOLLAND PROMOTIONS

Harry Holland has been active in the boxing world since he was a schoolboy, when his prowess earned him the Junior ABA Championship. He contined this early promising career to take the Senior ABA Championship (South West Division).

At the age of 26, his attention was drawn by an advertisement for a trainer to school the under-17's at the Hogarth Club, Chiswick. Although the position was originally for a limited period, Harry liked the job so much, and such was the success of his "stable", that he stayed to train winners in every Amateur Championship throughout the UK and Europe in both junior and senior divisions.

In 1982 Harry turned professional with a small stable that included 3 Southern Area Title Holders: Rocky Kelly, Gary Hobbs and Micky Harrison. He then concentrated on enlarging his stable while successfully promoting "everything except a World Title fight" in the UK.

The decision earlier this year to join Winners Worldwide Ltd was based on the "new dimension" that the combined companies' skills could offer boxing promotion in the UK, Europe & USA.

Harry currently runs his Gym at Ealing Northern Sports Centre, Sudbury Hill, helped by main assistant trainer John Bloomfield. With sixteen fighters under their guidance, six of whom are in the "Top Ten" in the UK and Southern Area Champions Rocky Kelly and Trevor Smith. Harry Holland and Winners Worldwide aim to make a significant impression in the boxing world this year, and have set their sights on promoting a world title fight in the not too distant future.

Halesmere House • 59 Islington Park Street • London N1 1QB
Tel: 01-354 3414 • Fax: 01-704 0213

•

71 Beech Road • Bedfont • Middlesex
Tel: 01-890 4030

HARRY HOLLAND PROMOTIONS

COST OF SHOW MONTI CARLO

WORLD MIDDLEWEIGHT CONTEST

Michael Nunn   v   Christopher Tiozzo
   (USA)   (France)

                                             £750,000

WORLD CRUISERWEIGHT CONTEST

GLEN McCrory } ? England
Patrick Lumaba }   Kenya

                                             £100,000

EUROPEAN MIDDLEWEIGHT CONTEST

Nigel Benn (England) v O/N	
Three other fights	£250,000
Advertising	£ 17,000
Printing	£ 10,000
Stewards	£ 10,000
Officials etc.	£ 6,000
+ Sundries	£ 3,000
Total Pay Out	£ 10,000
	£1m.156,000

APPROX. INCOME FROM SHOW MONTI CARLO

£20,000 outdoor venue

2,400 Ringside	at £200	
20 Rows of 30 each side of ring		£480,000
2,400 seats	at £150	
2,400 seats	at £100	£360,000
2,400 seats	at £ 75	£240,000
10,400 seat	at £ 50	£180,000
Total from Venue		£520,000
		£1780,000

British T.V. }	
World Wide TV }	
Sponsorship etc. }	£100,000
& merchandicing }	
	£1200.000
Pay/out	£3080.000
Profit on Sell Out (approx)	1156.000
	£1m:924.000

WINNERS WORLDWIDE IN ASSOCIATION WITH TOP RANK INC.

Top Rank, Inc.

NO SURRENDER!
INTERNATIONAL BOXING

BENN IS BACK!
NIGEL BENN v ROBBIE SIMS (U.S.A.)
(PEOPLES CHAMPION)   (NEVER BEEN STOPPED, NEVER BEEN DROPPED)

WEDNESDAY 3rd APRIL 1991
NEC ARENA BIRMINGHAM

DOORS 7.30pm, Commences 8pm

TICKETS: £150, £100, £50, £20, £10.

NEC BOX OFFICE: 021 780 4133 · CREDIT CARD BOOKINGS: 071 587 1414
BIRMINGHAM: BRMB / WAY AHEAD, BULLRING CENTRE · NOTTINGHAM: WAY AHEAD · COVENTRY: POSTER PLACE
MANCHESTER: PICCADILLY AGENCY · LIVERPOOL: BARNES TRAVEL · SHEFFIELD: CAVENDISH TRAVEL
HANLEY – STOKE – STAFFORD – WOLVERHAMPTON: MIKE LLOYD MEGASTORE,
AND ALL BRANCHES OF TICKETMASTER & KEITH PROWSE
ALL TICKETS SUBJECT TO BOOKING FEE

LAWRENCE GRAHAM

Our Ref: CCB/cja/B2734-1

Your Ref:

24th April 1992

Dear Sir,

Nigel Benn -v- Robbie Sims: Bethnal Green - 4.4.91

We act for Nigel Benn who fought the above contest which the British Boxing Board of Control Limited stated was promoted by yourself. We had requested from the Board a copy of the contract entered into between the promoter and our client, Mr Benn, but the Board advise that no contract was lodged with them and that we should refer to you for details of the contract. We accordingly would ask you to let us have a copy of the contract and in so far as the purse is concerned, confirmation that the sum was paid following the fight or if not, what sum was so paid, to whom and when?

We look forward to hearing from you at your earliest convenience.

Yours faithfully,

LAWRENCE GRAHAM

cc. N Benn, Esq.

190 STRAND, LONDON WC2R 1JN.   TELEPHONE: 071-379 0000. FAX: 071-379 6854. TELEX: 22673. DX: 39 LDE.
ALSO AT 1 SEETHING LANE, LONDON EC3N 4AX AND IN NEW YORK.

SOLICITORS, AUTHORISED BY THE LAW SOCIETY TO CONDUCT INVESTMENT BUSINESS

WINNERS

W O R L D W I D E
ADVERTISING LTD

THE DIRECTORS - WINNERS WORLWIDE LIMITED

Paul Woolf is an accomplished and well respected member of the legal profession, who combines proven skills in the tough world of law with a notable commercial flair. His prodigious energy and sophisticated analytical capabilities have earned him a reputation as a highly successful champion on behalf of his many clients in the sports and entertainment profession. He is well accquainted with the media world and is a man who will not allow his acknowledged integrity to compromise an aggressive, unrelenting approach on clients behalf.

Paul Crockford has a reputation in the music business as a man with a sharp eye for talent. He manages some of the most successful bands on the music scene today, including Level 42 and the Blow Monkeys. In fact, what Paul Crockford doesn't know about entertainment you could fit in the hole of one of their records. He has a specialist knowledge of arranging concerts, tours and steering his artists through the labyrinth of pop music small print.

Ross Hemsworth is an expert in the field of sponsorship who has a wealth of valuable connections in the sports world - particularly football and boxing. After working in the music business, he joined The World Sports Corporation and was made director of their soccer operation. In a promotional and PR capacity he has worked with such top named as The Nolans, Chas & Dave, and has established an excellent reputation as a representative for some of sports top stars

WINNERS WORLDWIDE
ADVERTISING LIMITED
REGISTERED OFFICE
HALESMERE HOUSE
59 ISLINGTON PARK ST
L O N D O N N 1 1 Q B
TEL: 01 354 3414
FAX: 01 704 0213
REG. IN ENGLAND 2366319

**WINNERS WORLDWIDE
ADVERTISING LTD**

WINNERS HAVE ARRIVED!

Winners Worldwide Limited represents a unique combination of skill and talent designed to bring a new dimension to the world of sports and entertainment promotion. Covering every aspect of this enormous growth area, the company is fully committed to the principle of winning on every front.

From management and sponsorship - Winners have acted for Sylvester Mittee and Linford Christie amongst others - to neogotiating transfer contracts (the most recent being Dalian Atkinson's signing from Ipswich to Sheffield Wednesday), the company has already gained a reputation for a fair, no-nonsense approach to these sometimes complex activities.

The acquistion of Fisher Athletic Football Club - where it is hoped the injection of new management skills will take the Club to the First Division - and the recent highly successful promotion of Championship Boxing in South London are further proof that Winners have the right formula.

But it does not stop there. Winners Worldwide will be applying the same expertise to their plans for the immediate future, which include not only football and atheltics throughout Europe, but also snooker events and championships boxing at the Albert Hall.

Winners Worldwide Advertising Ltd provides the resource and material back-up to the fast moving parent company. Co-Directors Jim Brooker and Steve Jones have over 35 years experience between them in every aspect of Advertising, PR, Promotions and Print Production. As part of the Winners team, they and their staff are fully committed to anticipating and servicing the company's publicity needs.

Apart from the company's " in-house " activities, however, Winners Worldwide Advertising have their own stable of clients covering a wide range of disciplines, from industrial to hi-tech consumer, all of whom add to an interesting portfolio for future development.

Winners Worlwide aim to be just that.

WINNERS WORLDWIDE
ADVERTISING LIMITED
REGISTERED OFFICE
HALESMERE HOUSE
59 ISLINGTON PARK ST
LONDON N1 1QB
TEL: 01 354 3414
FAX: 01 704 0213
REG. IN ENGLAND 2366319

Blazer's

Windsor, Berkshire
Telephone (07535) 56222

COPY

11th November 1982

Mr. Frank Warren and Mr. Harry Holland
28 Danbury Road
London W.1.

Dear Frank and Harry,

Following a recent Board Meeting on the subject of
Boxing at Blazer's, it has been decided that there
shall be no further Boxing at Blazer's at least for
a time.

Whilst the Boxing evenings are successful in terms of
support, they bring a type of customer who is quite
alien to the Blazer's operation and I know you will
appreciate that Blazer's being in a Royal Borough and
only a stone's throw from Windsor Castle itself has
to be very careful with the type of evening that it
puts on and we endeavour to keep a very low profile
at all times. We find this very difficult to do when
having a Boxing evening as they fall into two categories -
either knife edge all of the evening or all-out aggravation,
neither of which can be tolerated at Blazer's.

Please rest assured that if we do decide to resurrect Boxing
at Blazer's, perhaps in a year or so, you will be the first
to be contacted as I have always found both of you
excellent organisers and promoters but unfortunately the
incidents that took place at the last Boxing show have
resulted in the Board making this decision. Those
incidents were, if you like, 'just one of those things'
but, as already stated, something that we cannot possibly
let happen again in the future.

With very best wishes.

Yours sincerely,

S.G. Savva
Director & General Manager

Proprietors: Adengrove Productions Limited
Registered Office: 3 Pump Court, London EC1
Registered No. 1167063
VAT Registration No. 302 2395 02

Directors: P. Cowan, M.C.A. Cowan
Secretary: G.B.W. Walsh

Harry Holland Promotions
present

on Friday 26th February

At The Heathrow Park Hotel
Bath Road, Longford (near Morleys Health Club)

*A Professional Boxing Dinner & Dance
and Cabaret with top comedian*

Mike Reid
of Eastenders fame

4 Big Fights Featuring
• Nicky O'Dore • Nicky Bardle •
• Brian Gentry • Dave Baptiste •

in the

☆ British Masters - Boxing Championships ☆
☆ 3 Course Dinner ☆ Disco by Top Trax ☆

Reception: 6.30pm
Dinner: 7.30pm
Carriages: 1.30am

Personal appearances by stars of
"Eastenders" and **"The Bill"**
Plus World Boxing Champions
(Work permitting)

Tickets £60 inclusive

Tel: 0181 867 0435   Mobile: 0956 607 226
or any of the Boxers above

Harry serves up a cracker

I WISH to congratulate "Winners Worldwide" and Harry Holland for their excellent 'value for money' show at the Battersea Town Hall on June 6. Seven contests is a rarity nowadays, but they proved it could be done and were rewarded with, I hope, a full house.

Serg Fame and Derek Myers served up a tremendous 10 round contest in which Serg retained his Southern Area light-heavyweight title. It was a non-stop action fight from first bell to last and although I made Fame a much clearer winner than referee Larry O'Connell, it couldn't detract from an epic encounter. Serg and Derek, you were marvellous.

The atmosphere generated by the Andy Till and Ensley Bingham bout had to be felt to be believed and here again it was grade one stuff from the off.

Andy, I am sorry to say, let his demonic will to win rule his head and I thought he deserved to be disqualified for flagrant use of his elbow on his opponent's neck or back.

I have seen every one of Till's fights, either live or on video and I cannot find fault with his heart, stamina or fitness.

In these respects I admire him tremendously, but he should surely have learned by now to curb his enthusiasm in the ring.

It's alright wanting to win, but you have to remember not to park the rules at the gate every time you go out and Andy, incidentally, you are in a boxing match, not World War III.

Tony Collins has been very lucky so far, not to be disqualified for taking 'pot-shots' at fallen opponents. Andy you were not so lucky, I hope you learn by it.

Trevor Smith and Roland Ericsson, who are good enough to top any small show in the country, won supporting bouts, and there were three well matched six rounders as well. Once again, I say 'Well done'. How about next season Andy Till v John Davies, Roland Ericsson v Paul McCarthy, Derek Myers v Jimmy Peters, Johnny B. Good v Steve Walker? — now there's a bill. Yours in sport — B. Kempster, Wix's Lane, Clapham, SW4.

FAME catches Myers with a right but their fortunes swayed throughout the exciting 10 rounder at Battersea.

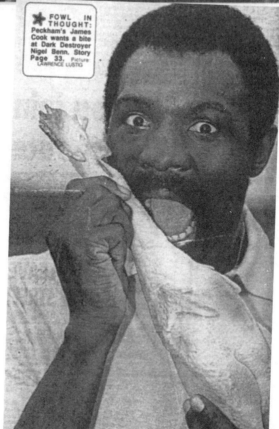

★ FOWL IN THOUGHT: Peckham's James Cook wants a bite at Dark Destroyer Nigel Benn. Story Page 33. Picture LAWRENCE LUSTIG

Faces of iron: Andy Till is flanked by his manager Harry Holland and (right) trainer Johnny Bloomfield

PHIL SHEPHARD-LEWIS

Till a throwback to bare-knuckle days

By Steve Bunce

FEW boxers look as mean and determined as British light-middleweight champion Andy Till, who defends his title for the second time when he meets Wally Swift at the Royal Albert Hall tonight.

His face is a simple reminder of what bare-knuckle bruisers looked like. F.W.J. Henning, a 19th-century ring historian, might have been describing Till when he wrote of one prize fight: "Iron fists fell on iron faces."

Heavy brows, which cast a shadow of mangled flesh over his cold eyes, the stoic jaw and cropped hair combine to make the Middlesex milkman a menacing spectacle. Till, 29, developed his skills over seven years from fighting in boxing's small halls.

Last September, Till's supporters packed into Watford Town Hall to watch him beat Swift for the second time to win the British title. Victory tonight means the Lonsdale Belt for Till. He is an honest boxer who has been hurt by unknown fighters in forgotten brawls, and disqualified during a title eliminator for illegal use of the elbow.

He has taken part in numerous "fights of the night", including his first meeting with Swift when £58 in nobbins (coins and notes) — the sport's traditional show of respect — littered the ring. "I get annoyed when fighters like Chris Eubank get all the glory," said Till, whose first defence was in December, when he stopped Tony Collins in three rounds. "I've worked my guts out to get where I am now."

Till, a father of three, works hard at a time when too many young hopefuls make the mistake of turning professional too early in their career. "Every morning I get up at 4.30, get to the yard by 5 and I'm out delivering by 5.30. Every day, in rain, snow and freezing conditions."

He is back in the yard by 11 to complete the same routine he has been following for eight years. "I do it because it is my security," he said. "But nobody *wants* to get up at 4.30 to deliver milk."

TILL DEATH US DO PART

by Glyn Leach

Manager Harry Holland was at the end of his tether as he watched his boxer, Andy Till, throw away the chance of a shot at British light-middleweight champion Gary Stretch, by getting disqualified for illegal use of the elbow against Manchester's Ensley Bingham, in the third round of their British title final eliminator at Battersea Town Hall, last week. Hard-man Till, the Southern Area champion, has been waiting to get a crack at glamour-boy Stretch for some time now, but all his hopes evaporated in a few moments of madness. A perturbed Harry told *Boxing Weekly*:

"There can be no excuse for that. Andy threw it away - it was crazy, blatant madness. I tried to ease him up a bit between rounds, but he was so worked up, the situation just got too much for him and he lost control. I was calling him every name under the sun, but I just couldn't get through to him. The worst thing about it is that Andy was outboxing Bingham at the time, and I wasn't really expecting that, although I knew that he would be the stronger man. Andy told me that he thought that he was badly cut, and that he wanted to try and knock Bingham out, but trying to do it with your elbow is a going a little bit too far.

None too pleased . . . Harry Holland reads the riot act to Andy Till

Pic Action Images

"Tilly certainly didn't do his public image that much good, because he's a lovely bloke really - the sort that would do anything for you. It all just got on top of him because he had so many problems in the build-up to this fight.

"He's been suffering with small fractures to bones in his feet, the result of him doing his training runs on concrete. He was on pain-killers for ages, but he had to stop taking them about five weeks ago, or else he wouldn't have been allowed to fight. He was getting some "natural" treatment for the injuries, and it seemed to be working quite well, but

he was still in pain.

"Then, just as he had to stop taking the pain-killers, he had his nose split in sparring by Serg Fame, so that ruled out any proper fight training in the run-up to this one. I had to put him on the pads for the last five weeks of preparation.

"But he's a great bloke, and I love working with him, and, although he was talking about packing it all in after the fight, I reckon he'll change his mind, and I'll be looking to get him a shot at the winner between Stretch and Bingham next season. He won't be so silly again."

Know what I mean, Harry?

Boxing's Mr. Big packs a punch for Hounslow

FEATURE BY RON LEWIS

THERE'S a reason for the big smile on Harry Holland's face these days, for after ten years in the boxing business he can reasonably say that he has cracked it.

While West London has never been the cockpit of boxing which South or East London is, Harry has worked tirelessly to make himself one of the major players in British boxing.

For after ten years Harry sees himself as being on the verge of producing his first national champion.

Harry said: "Unlike ten years ago, there are lots of promoters but not that many champions.

"Now, more than ever, it's important and produce champions because it means you can put on the best show."

Backing

For most of his time in the professional game Harry has gone without any major backing. Now he has the backing of Winners Worldwide promotion—though he still

his home in Beech Road, Bedfont.

Harry boxed as an amateur himself, but had no involvement with the game for many years as he worked to bring up three young children.

He never lost the boxing bug and took up coaching at Chiswick's Hogarth amateur club ten years ago.

When the time came for some of his young talent to turn professional, he decided to join the paid game as well.

Two of the first string of fighters made Harry's name as a manager Gary Hobbs and Rocky Kelly.

The progression of middleweight Hobbs was quick. He won the Southern area title and was on the verge of a British Title fight when a shocking accident at work left Gary blind in one eye and finished his career.

Kelly's exciting all-action

performed to a packed.

Kelly twice won the Southern Area title and twice challenged for the British Title—against Kirkland Laing—but without success.

Collapsed

But it was one of Kelly's fights that brought Harry's blackest day as a manager and promoter. Welter opponent Steve Watt collapsed and died after a fight in 1986.

Harry has a cold recollection of those three days when Steve tottered between life and death on a life-support machine.

He...

tion was to say 'that's it's not worth it.'

"But then I sat down with some of my fighters and realised it was a selfish attitude, and I wasn't considering them.

"After all it was because of them that I went into managing and promoting.

Harry now sees his immediate prospects as the best they have ever been.

Two fighters, Trevor Smith and Andy Straughn, have recently picked up British and Commonwealth Titles without success, but three more fighters are set to challenge for the British title in close future.

Harry has three current Southern Area champions as well—welterweight

Andy Till and lightheavyweight Surge Fame.

Harry is also getting the better of his matches with top manager Terry Lawless.

"My boys have won four out of five bout against his fighters.

"Rocky Kelly box unbeaten David Dew, Andy Till beat W. O. Wilson, Trevor Smith beat Mickey Hughes, and recently Surge Fame flattened Johnny Graham in one round."

But Harry is quick to admit he could not have made it all on his own and is the person he thanks most is close friend and trainer Johnny Bloomfield.

"We've been together since the start and hope fully we will soon have our first title.

• Taking it on the chin. Harry is flanked by boxers Surge Fame (left) and Andy Till with trainer Johnny Bloomfield in support

---

Trevor's title shot

By DEAN JONES

BOXER Trevor Smith caused an upset in a British title eliminator and declared afterwards: "The champ is there for the taking."

Smith, the 25-year-old Southern Area Champion, is being lined up for a fight against British welterweight title holder Kirkland Laing after he stopped Mickey Hughes at Battersea last week.

The title eliminator — and Smith's defence of Southern Area title — ended in the sixth round when the 27-year-old Hughes, who fought for Britain in the Los Angeles Olympic Games, was adjudged to be no longer capable of defending himself, following a series of blows from the Little Hallingbury boxer.

Smith's manager Harry Holland and promotion agency Winners' Worldwide are now starting negotiations with Mickey Duff, Laing's manager, for a title shot, possibly before Christmas.

If the Laing negotiations break down, Smith's management is looking for a fight against the European champion, Nino La Rocha of Italy.

Of Laing, Smith said: "He is getting on a bit in boxing terms. He is 35 now and he is not as good as he was.

"He still is going to be awkward but I think he is ready to be taken."

At Battersea, Smith was ahead on points when the fight was stopped, winning four of the five rounds.

The former Eastern Counties' champion was not unduly troubled by a fighter who had knocked out 15 of his 19 opponents and was being tipped as next British champion.

Smith hurt Hughes with a left hook in the second round and opened up a cut on his eye.

The eye wound opened up again in the sixth.

Smith said: "The eye was bleeding really badly. I hit him again with a left hook, which made his legs buckle again.

"Then I just fired shots with the left and the right. They kept catching him and he was all over the place.

"The referee jumped in because he was defenceless."

Smith, formerly an ABA semi-finalist, has had 12 knock-outs in an unbeaten run of 15 fights.

The former Norwood boxer said: "I fought how I predicted I would fight. I could not do a thing wrong that night. It was a good performance."

• TREVOR SMITH ... a title chance at last.

Boxing sorts out the bullies

By Teresa Castle

BULLYING can cause many problems for young children but Harry Holland dealt with it in his own way – he learnt to box.

Harry, 50, from Feltham is now a well known boxing manager and promoter.

"When I was 11 I first became interested in boxing because I was being bullied. I am a firm believer that it is a great character builder especially for shy people."

He feels it is total rubbish that boxing makes people more violent and said if anything it teaches them discipline and simply gives them self confidence – but added it must be taught by proper instructors.

"When it is taught by a proper instructor who knows what he is doing it is one of the best sports boys can learn.

"For me boxing gave me a lot of confidence but it did not mean I went around hitting people. Bullies don't last long in a boxing ring because it means going up against someone their own size."

Harry, now a father of three, joined a club after becoming hooked on boxing and spent a few years in the ring.

By the time he was 26 he decided to have a break but then became involved in training children how to box.

Through his boxing career he has helped fighters gain numerous titles from Southern area championships to British and European championships. In fact the only one he has not promoted is a world title.

But at the moment he has more press-

ing things to deal with as he is about to fulfil his lifetime ambition which is to promote a fight at the Albert Hall.

It is a joint promotion and the fight is between Andy Till and Wally Swift for the Lonsdale Belt.

The fight is on April 14 and will place the two fighters back in the ring for the first time since Andy won the British title from Wally last year.

For Harry boxing is his life and he can not understand people who call for the sport to be banned or say it is too aggressive.

"Men are aggressive by nature and they will fight but what I can't stand is why people always have a go at boxing.

"Why not have a go at football because heading a ball can kill more brain cells than a punch in the boxing ring."

As long as the rules are obeyed the danger is greatly reduced, he added.

But one thing which he agrees does put a shadow over the game is promoters who do not ensure their fighters are evenly matched.

"Fights which are over in the first or second round are no fun for anyone to watch and if the fighters are not evenly matched there is more chance someone will get hurt."

In the future, apart from achieving his lifetime ambition, Harry would also like to promote a world title and is also interested in acting.

He has done extra work on a number of television programmes from Grange Hill to Eastenders either just as a walk on part or will a couple of lines and he finds that great fun.

■ KID GLOVES: Harry Holland with star fighter Andy Stoneface Till.

Club's a knock-out .... Young boxers at the Hogarth Boxing Club await the Round One bell at the Hogarth Youth Centre, Chiswick during the club's annual presentation evening twenty five years ago. Harry Holland, joint trainer at the club with Colin Cracknell, stated at the event that there were possible Olympic champions among the fighting fit group. Was any of that potential undisputedly fulfilled? On the night 16 year old London Champion Robin Cox, Best Achiever at the club was floored with flu. but runner-up Grantley Beckles picked up his award.

HARRY PACKS A PUNCH

BEDFONT boxing promoter Harry Holland is grooming Cranford fighter Andy Till towards a championship challenge later this year.

Harry, who will be ringside tonight (Thursday) for the latest of his fight nights, has tipped light middleweight Andy for the top.

REPORT BY ROBERT SCOTT HALTER

The boxing supremo, who lives in Kendall Close, told Chronicle Sport: "Andy is the most successful of my current fighters and we are looking towards a WBC International Light Middleweight title fight when the time is right."

But tonight the spotlight will be on Joe Bugner Junior, who aims to follow in dad's footsteps and takes on John Harwood of Newcastle in a heavyweight bout. The Bugner fight is on the undercard of Harry's latest presentation at Battersea Town Hall.

Topping the bill is a Southern Area Middleweight title fight between Lester Jacobs of Peckham and Tony Burke, the champion, from Croydon.

Since he last appeared on the Chronicle Sport pages seven years ago, Harry has seen his first British and European champion, James Cook, join rival manager Mickey Duff.

"If luck had been on my side, I could have had at least two other British champions by now," said Holland, referring to welterweight Trevor Smith and light heavyweight Serg Fame.

The quality of the fighters that Holland has produced from his gym at The Ealing Northern Sports Centre has been a result of the expertise of his long time trainer, John Bloomfield.

He said: "I'd really like to thank Johnny for his great support and I am delighted to see that he has been rewarded for his hard work by being a corner man for all of Frank Bruno's next fights."

Away from boxing, Holland is best known as a film extra and regularly appears in popular TV shows such as Eastenders and The Bill. One of his most recent roles was a security officer in the mini serial Love Hurts.

To help raise money for charity, he has even been brave enough to parachute from a plane at 13,000 feet — which he described as his most exciting experience.

His family are most important to him and Holland has three grown-up children and is presently expecting his third grandchild.

As a keen reader of the Middlesex Chronicle, Holland had a special message to any of you wishing to come to one of his shows.

He said: "I think the Chronicle is an excellent local paper and I get it every week so I am going to give a bit of an incentive. Anyone that comes along to one of my shows with a copy of the Middlesex Chronicle under their arm will get 10% off.

"Get behind Harry Holland promotions, come and see the show and have a fantastic evening and I am sure that you will want to come again.

"Those that have not been boxing should give it a chance and if you can honestly say afterwards that you did not get value for money, return your admission price and you can't get fairer than that."

Chris Ellison (above), has left *The Bill*'s DI Burnside behind to play a sports promoter in *Ellington* (Wednesday ITV) — and he has some impressive sporting connections himself. "I know quite a few sports promoters and managers personally, such as boxing's Frank Warren, Harry Holland, Frank Maloney, and a number of international sportsmen including snooker player Jimmy White — who plays himself in the film — and former heavyweight boxing champion Lennox Lewis."

The drama was created specially for him and he thinks it should make a series. "Perhaps Lennox can guest in a future episode," he says.

Harry's on a downer!

LOCAL boxing promoter Harry Holland admits he is terrified of heights, and yet in just over two weeks he will be free falling 12,000 feet or three miles, for charity.

Harry heard that a local scout group were urgently in need of funds: "They were urgently in need of funds: "They wnat to buy a 12 seater coach to take the kids out and about and I thought I could help them raise money."

Being a plucky fellow, Harry an ex-lightweight-heavyweight boxer who fought Richard Dury – a man who went on to fight the great Muhammed Ali for the world title – decided upon a feat that would unlock his deepest fears.

"It's the fact that I am absolutely terrified of heights that made me choose parachuting, I thought it would attract more attention and raise more money, who knows I could overcome my fear of heights."

Harry, 46, had never parachuted before: "Even climbing upstairs makes me giddy," he confessed, but he says has not had to complete any specific training."

"When you free fall, you usually land on your feet and I'll be jumping tied to an instructor who will help me if I encounter any difficulties.

But Harry is still apprehensive: "I will be heading for the ground at speeds approaching 140mph, I am nervous already!"

He's been in boxing since the age of 11 as boxer, manager, training and now promoter and has always been a fit man: "I'm a fitness fanatic, one of my hobbies is sub-aqua diving."

Donations are pouring in to Harry for the sponsored free fall which will take place over the Cambridgeshire country-side on October l: "I've received £140 in pledges already in one day," he said.

But he needs as much money as possible: "Anyone who wants to sponser me can phone 890 4030 any time. All donations, no matter how small will help."

Harry added: "I'm just very determined and there is no way I will back out now, I just hope I get down in one piece!" So do we.

Audley is star guest

OLYMPIC champion Audley Harrison proved a big hit when he dropped in to offer some advice to aspiring boxers last Thursday.

The Brunel University graduate, who is unbeaten in the heavyweight ranks, popped along to the gym at the back of the North Star pub in Whitton Road, Hounslow, to see the youngsters, aged eight to 15, in action and hand out some advice.

And if they turn out to be half as successful as he has, then no one will be complaining.

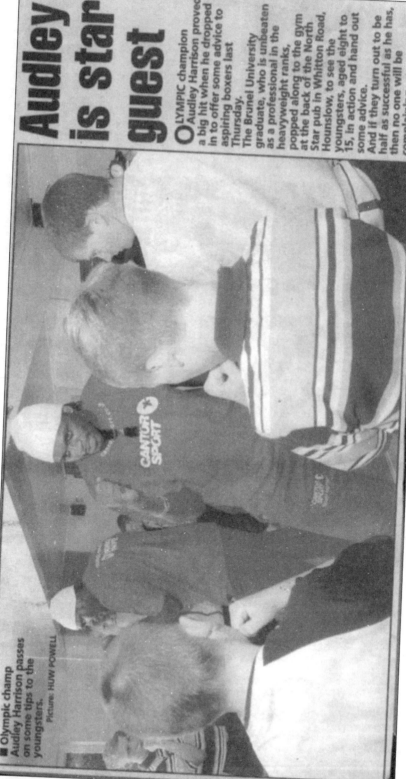

■ Olympic champ Audley Harrison passes on some tips to the youngsters.
Picture: HUW POWELL

Standard Picture: DAVID CASEY

IN CONTROL . . . Rocky Kelly (right) on the way to a fifth-round win over Paul Murray at Battersea Town Hall.

Kelly steps up British title challenge

A WEEK IN BOXING

by Boxing Weekly Editor Ian Probert

■ A funny thing happened last Thursday night — I went to a London boxing show and enjoyed every minute of it! Practically every fight on the bill was evenly matched; there was a distinct lack of over-the-hill Mexican imports; there was atmosphere; and every fan left the arena satisfied that their entrance fee was money well spent. The only thing missing? Television cameras to record one of the most exciting promotions staged this year.

The show in question was "Battle of Battersea VIII", promoted by Harry Holland and Winners Worldwide, held at Battersea Town Hall. And it is ironic that at a time when the sport drastically needs to show to its increasingly critical followers that it is capable of generating genuine excitement, a show like this is ignored by national TV.

Harry Holland is a fair man who tries to ensure that the fans get their money's worth. He often operates at a loss and for a show like "Battle VIII" which featured seven exciting fights, this can be heartbreaking. So often TV fight audiences are served up the same old recipe of a rising British prospect knocking out a flabby, inept fighter import in one or two rounds, when the real fights, between real fighters who actually want to compete are ignored.

If you want to see boxing at its best get yourself a ticket for Harry Holland's next promotion. Details of which will appear in a forthcoming issue of *Boxing Weekly.*

THE **20** MOST IMPORTANT MEN IN BOXING

by Tony Roberts

British boxing is going through a bad time at the moment. Successive losses in world title fights by Lloyd Honeyghan; Johnny Nelson; Michael Watson; Glenn McCrory; Jim McDonnell; and Billy Hardy have left the sport in a pretty bedraggled state. But help is at hand.

Listed below are twenty of the sport's biggest names, people who have the future of boxing in their hands. The list is by no means comprehensive, and in no particular order, but in *Boxing Weekly's* view, these are the names which hold the key to British boxing's ultimate success.

Jarvis Astaire

Has a substantial stake in Wembley Stadium and works closely with Mickey Duff and Terry Lawless. Has promoted some of this country's biggest fights. A shrewd businessman.

Mike Barrett

A familiar figure in the fight game. A former partner of Mickey Duff, and a well-travelled and knowledgeable fight aficionado. Has promoted over 150 shows at London's Albert Hall and up until last year looked set to grab a firm foot-hold in the upper echelons of world boxing with prospects Gary Jacobs and Derek Williams. Jacobs was only a fight or two away from a world title shot, but successive losses to Buddy McGirt and Donovan Boucher have forced the Glaswegian to take a trip back to the drawing-board. More was expected of

Mickey Duff

The man whom the American's call: the "Smartest Cookie" in boxing. A deep thinker and eloquent talker, friends and enemies alike grudgingly acknowledge his considerable knowledge and experience of the game. Has produced no less than six world champions since commencing his career as a matchmaker in his early twenties. His influence on the sport over the years is immeasurable. Lately however, times have not been easy for him, with consecutive losses in world title fights involving Duke McKenzie; Lloyd Honeyghan; Michael Watson; and John Mugabi. He's sure to rebound though, with a young and rising stable which includes the likes of Henry Akinwande and the hard-hitting Henry Wharton.

Barney Eastwood

Canny Irish entrepreneur w the boxing scene in the mi his work with the charisma McGuigan. Has one of the the country, including seve Panamanian fighters.

Reg Gutteridge

Boxing's premier wit, and

Nigel Benn with flamboyant mentor Ambrose Mendy

Harry Holland

Works mainly in London, and in my opinion puts on the best boxing shows in the country. Has no big stars in his stable but his fighters are crowd pleasers of the highest standard. Is backed by the ambitious Winners Worldwide promotional group, a company who at present have promised far more than they've delivered. Has a genuine flair for matchmaking but

Gary Newbon

Played top-class Rugby for Rosslyn Park in between working for local newspapers. Joined Westward TV in Plymouth, fronting the local sports programme before graduating to Central TV and eventually becoming controller of sport at the station. Styles himself as boxing's premier fight interrogator. (Judge his performance after the recent Johnny Nelson-Carlos DeLeon debacle). One to watch.

Frank Maloney

The man most likely to? The answer to the

LIFE

IT'S SOMETIMES SAD AND MAKES US CRY

AND MAKES ONE FEEL WE CAN ALMOST DIE

THEN SOMETHING HAPPENS TO MAKE US CHEER

AND WANT TO LIVE ANOTHER YEAR

THE YEARS GO BY AND WE GROW OLD

AND BEGIN TO LISTEN TO WHAT WE ARE TOLD

IF ONLY WE HAD KNOWN BEFORE

WHAT TROUBLES AND STRIFE LIFE HAD IN STORE

THE GOOD THE BAD THE HAPPY THE SAD

OH WHAT HAPPINESS WE HAVE HAD

THE TEARS OF DESPAIR THAT WILL SOON DISAPPEAR

OH GOD LET US HOPE WE LIVE TO MANY A YEAR

TO FEEL THE SUN UPON OUR FACE

AND NOT TO LEAVE THIS WORLD IN DISGRACE

FOR THAT'S THE WAY IT'S MEANT TO BE

A LIFE FULL OF HURT AND HARMONY.

(LIFE-HARRY HOLLAND)

T H E   F I G H T E R .

He may be strong and very brave

A man that will suffer not any Knave,

He will fight many a foe

Even though six foot tall, from head to toe.

They will punch him, but he'll not go down

Because he's done many a round in tougher a town.

His heart is big, as big as can be

With a punch to fell men as big as a tree.

And when his nose starts to bleed

He'll wipe it away and take no heed

And as rounds go on and he starts to slow

Also His opponent thinks it's time to show.

He'll slip his jab and throw one hammer blow

To register once again, that almighty K.O.

And as he stands with arms held high

So proud he is, and not so shy

For fighter he is come what may

FINAL
And till the bell, he die some day.

HARRY HOLLAND   1989

M Y   C H I L D R E N

OF THEM I AM SO PROUD - I WANT TO SING THEIR PRAISES OH SO LOUD,

THE WAY THEY CAME THROUGH LIFE SO WELL,

EVEN THOUGH AT TIMES IT SEEMED LIKE HELL.

TO LIVE WITH ME WHEN I AM BAD,

TO SEE ME SMILE WHEN I AM GLAD.

THEY WILL ALWAYS BE A COMFORT TO - EVEN WHEN I AM FEELING BLUE,

OF MY MANDY - A GIRL SO TRUE - A TOWER OF STRENGTH,

TO BE WITH YOU.

MY JOHN - WHO'S GROWN TO SUCH A`LAD, THAT I AM SO PROUD

TO BE CALLED ▮▮▮ DAD.

THE DAUGHTER TRACY - FULL OF BEANS

SURELY A FATHERS DREAM OF DREAMS.

FOR THAT IS THE REASON WHY I AM HERE,

TO LOVE AND CHERISH FROM YEAR TO YEAR

THE CHILDREN THAT I LOVE SO DEAR!

HARRY HOLLAND - 28.03.1989

F R I E N D S .

When things go well they're always there

To treasure with you, things in life to share,

And when life is not going so well

It is a pleasure to have friends to call Pal.

When life is full of ups and downs

You need your friends and not the clowns!

There'll always be people to put you down

But friends they'll be, to rally round

And as life goes from year to year

We'll raise our glasses and give a cheer

For the true friends that we love so dear.

HARRY HOLLAND   1989